Robert L. Woodson, Sr.

The Triumphs of Joseph

How Today's Community Healers Are Reviving Our Streets and Neighborhoods

T H E   F R E E   P R E S S
New York   London
Toronto   Sydney   Singapore

*f*P

THE FREE PRESS
A Division of Simon & Schuster Inc.
1230 Avenue of the Americas
New York, NY 10020

Designed by Pei Koay

Manufactured in the United States of America

10 9 8 7 6 5 4 3 2 1

Library of Congress Cataloging-in-Publication Data

Woodson, Robert L.
    The triumphs of Joseph : how today's community healers are
reviving our streets and neighborhoods / Robert L. Woodson.
        p.   cm.
    Includes bibliographical references.
    ISBN: 1-4165-6786-0
    ISBN 13: 978-1-4165-6786-8

    1. Community development, Urban—United States—Citizen
participation.   2. Volunteer workers in community development
—United States.   3. Volunteer workers in social service—United
States.   4. Inner cities—United States.   5. Urban poor—United
States.   6. Social action—United States.   I. Title.
HN90.C6W65   1998
307.1'416'0973—dc21   97-11493
                                                                  CIP

This book is dedicated to the hundreds of grassroots leaders I have had the privilege of knowing, who have each, in his or her own special way, touched and changed my life and the lives of the thousands of individuals they have served. Among these I would especially like to recognize Harriet Henson of Pittsburgh and the late Robert "Fat Rob" Allen—two courageous individuals who epitomize the commitment and power of our nation's "Josephs."

Contents

Acknowledgments

My deepest gratitude goes to all those who contributed to the evolution of this book over the past 30 years: those who envisioned the crucial role grassroots leaders would play in revitalizing our nation, those who helped articulate and document that vision, and above all, the thousands of committed men and women in America's low-income communities who have made that vision a reality and those who have so generously offered support to sustain and expand these efforts.

Special thanks go to the following trailblazers: Atron Gentry and his staff at the Westside Study Center in Pasadena, California, who introduced me to the concept of empowering community-based self-help initiatives; Sister Falaka Fattah, her husband David, and her son Chaka Fattah (now a United States Congressman), who embodied the concept of modern-day "Josephs" as, through their House of Umoja, they transformed hundreds of gang members in Philadelphia into righteous and responsible men, and Peter and Brigitta Berger, and Richard John Neuhaus, author of the landmark manifesto of effective social policy "To Empower People," whose rigorous academic research validated and promoted the efforts of grassroots healing agents.

I would also like to acknowledge the friends and colleagues who were with me during my tenure at the National Urban League, in particular Dr. Robert Hill and his research staff, who helped to shape my work and provided the basis of the first cost/benefit analysis of grassroots initiatives. I extend my gratitude to the late William J. Baroody, Sr., who had the vision and saw the importance of mediating institutions for public policy, and to all those who supported my work at the American Enterprise Institute (AEI), giving me an opportunity as a practitioner to travel, to reflect on my experiences, and to begin to introduce these ideas through the major media.

Heartfelt thanks go to all those who shared my vision and had the faith in the power of grassroots societal healing agents in the earliest, most vulnerable stages of the emergence of our nation's "Josephs," including the following: Charles White of the Charles Stewart Mott Foundation, who supported my efforts at AEI; Richard Larry and the Sarah Scaife Foundation; Joanne Beyer and the Scaife Family Foundation; Stephanie Lee and the Sunmark Foundation; Michael Joyce, Andrew "Tiny" Rader, and William Schambra of the Lynde and Harry Bradley Foundation, who recognized and supported the potential of the National Center for Neighborhood Enterprise when it was only a dream in my heart and who have stood fast as NCNE supporters; Jeremiah Milbank and Chris Olander and the JM Foundation; James Piereson and the John M. Olin Foundation, Inc.; Virginia Gilder; James V. Capua and the William H. Donner Foundation, Inc.; Mary Ross; and Joseph Dolan and the Achelis and Bodman Foundations.

My gratitude also goes to all of the staff at NCNE who have weathered the storms and have been a part of its whirlwind of activities during the past 16 years—especially my executive assistant Hattie Porterfield, who stood fast on the front lines and has been my intercessor with the world. Thanks also to David Caprara, Heather Humphries, Gwen Williams, Anne Miller, and Pam Taylor, friends and advisers through the years.

Pastor Lee Earl helped me to understand the Gospel in all its majesty and how its principles apply to everyday life. And thanks to Wilhelmina Bell-Taylor, whose friendship and guidance on so many fronts have kept my compass pointed in the right direction.

Without the tireless editorial support provided by Collette Caprara this book would have been an impossible task. She worked closely with me in the development of these ideas and helped me to think them through for publication.

And finally, my heartfelt thanks go to the members of my family, who provided the support and inspiration that have been crucial to our successful mission: my wife Ellen; my sons Ralph, Rob, and Jamal; my daughter Tanya; and the lights of my life, my grandchildren Arianna and Robert L. Woodson, III.

The
Triumphs
of
Joseph

Chapter 1

Dreams and Omens of Impending Doom

On June 25, 1996, Bill Griffin, age twenty-six, was ambushed in a drive-by shooting and became one of more than 350 young black men who are killed in street violence each year in our nation's capital. Black-on-black murders in Washington, D.C., have become so common that Griffin's death was newsworthy only because he was the last of his mother's four children to be murdered before the age of thirty.[1]

The day after Bill Griffin was killed, hundreds of miles away in a Milwaukee neighborhood two young girls, thirteen-year-old Lawanda Moore and her best friend, eleven-year-old Sholanda Young, were playing on a front porch when two cars came roaring down the street filled with young black men with guns blazing away at one another. Stray bullets took Lawanda's life and left Sholanda in a coma. Before patrol cars arrived at the crime scene, someone picked up the bullet shell casings and threw them into a sewer to prevent the police from gathering the evidence needed to track down the killers.

The pain in the heart of the mother in D.C. who has lost all four of her children and the pain and despair of the parents of those two little girls will be with them for the rest of their lives. I can identify with that pain and that agony, because members of my own family continue to reside in a high-crime, drug-infested neighborhood of Philadelphia, where two of my nephews have been stabbed and rushed to intensive care units. Recently, I was called upon to deliver the eulogy for another twenty-year-old nephew who had been murdered in front of his older brother and his fourteen-year-old brother. He had been shot once in the head and twice in the chest by a neighbor he had known all his life.

These tragic killings are just a handful of the more than nine thousand black-on-black homicides that are committed throughout the nation each year in a virtual reign of terror that has plagued the black community for more than a decade. These deaths were not caused by marauding bands of the Klan or lynching by a White Citizens Council. These victims were killed at the hands of their own people.

A virtual dance of death has become almost a part of the culture of inner-city communities. We have come to accept violence and our hearts have become calloused to its impact. Today, little children can stand at the scene of a homicide, eating ice cream cones. Unless they know the victim, there is no longer any horror or remorse. Each year, more blacks are killed in urban violence by other blacks than the total number of the blacks who died in service throughout the nine years of the Vietnam War.

Pastor Leonidas Young, a liberal Democrat, former mayor of Richmond, Virginia, and longtime civil rights advocate summarized our condition when he proclaimed, "The crisis now facing black America is more devastating than the combined impact of slavery, racial discrimination, and drugs. For now, the enemy is within."

Granted, racism is still a problem in the United States today, and a number of thinkers and sociologists, such as John Sibley Butler, have proposed workable strategies to adress this issue.[2] However, to continue to focus on racism as the principal enemy of the black community is to travel down a lethal path of self-deception. Our communities are dying from self-inflicted wounds. And the moral free-fall that is taking this tragic toll penetrates beyond all boundaries of race, ethnicity, and income level. The societal dissolution that is devastating our nation's low-income minority neighborhoods has begun to gnaw away at white, upper-income society. Black communities cannot place their hope for survival in demands for an end to racism and economic disparity.

If race and poverty were the root causes of societal disintegration, then why do we find the same widespread self-destruction occurring among the affluent? Carroll O'Connor, Gloria Vanderbilt, and other affluent celebrities have all felt the pain of losing a child to substance abuse or suicide. George McGovern's daughter, Terry, died a lonely alcoholic, frozen in the winter snow. Margaux Hemingway, supermodel and granddaughter of the famed author Ernest Hemingway, was found dead in her condominium after a long struggle with alcohol and bulimia. Her grandfather, as well as his father, brother, and sister had all committed suicide.

If race and economic disparity were the cause of social dysfunction, how is it that in a pastoral white community in Texas, a group of ten white boys surrounded a farm horse and tortured it to death and then showed no remorse as they bragged and joked in front of their horrified parents? If race and economic disadvantage were the cause of the crisis that confronts us, why do we have high-profile cases such as that of Eric and Lyle Menendez, brothers who gunned down their parents in a cold-blooded, premeditated act of murder as they watched television in their affluent suburban home? If economic disadvantage and a lack of educational opportunities were the cause of our crisis, if affluence and education were the solution, why didn't authorities assume that a Harvard degree would have prevented the accused Unabomber from calculating, with cool indifference, the cruel murders of his victims? Why didn't prestige and privilege prevent a Nobel laureate from sexually abusing the children he worked with? Why have so many Ph.D.s and M.D.s signed themselves in to the Betty Ford Clinic?

General trends among youths in our nation's suburban communities—rising rates of gang activity, youth crime, and adolescent substance abuse—provide evidence that the most critical problems of our society are not caused by poverty or racism and they cannot, therefore, be alleviated by remedies that assume these causes. In an affluent suburb of Virginia, for example, it was recently revealed that a year-long theft ring had been operated by the community's "cream of the crop"—popular and successful athletes and cheerleaders. The youths had habitually shoplifted items they could easily have paid for, and other suburban youths who were employed at the stores they robbed were accessories to their thefts, removing merchandise detectors from merchandise and providing fake receipts.

Societal disintegration within our nation's inner cities is not an isolated anomaly. Conditions in urban areas provide a barometer for conditions in American society at large. We are facing a nationwide crisis—a spiritual and moral free-fall—which has brought fear and uncertainty throughout America. Fifty-three percent of respondents in a recent USA Today/CNN/Gallup Poll said that the nation's moral problems concerned them more than economic problems, while 39 percent rated the state of moral values in our nation as "very weak."[3]

The good news is that solutions to this crisis do exist. But if we are to tap the possibilities for moral and spiritual revitalization, we must move the focus of the policy debate beyond racial and economic considerations. For an answer to the crisis we now face we must go beyond the level of education, jobs, housing, or racial reconciliation. These strategies will never be able to address the root of a crisis that is essentially spiritual and moral. If we are to identify effective remedies, we must be willing to look to a new source for solutions.

In the arena of medicine where the stakes are literally life and death, we scurry to any signs of hope for cures for rampant diseases. We are focused on the effectiveness of a remedy, regardless of its source. Not long ago, the *Wall Street Journal* featured a story on a new cancer drug that was developed by a Chinese yogurt company.[4] We did not ask whether the yogurt people had medical degrees and experience. We asked only what impact their product had on the devastating disease. If we are to discover a solution to a societal disease that is just as widespread, lethal, and uncontrollable as cancer, we must be willing to exhibit this same openness to unconventional experts.

Today, among the ruins of inner-city neighborhoods, there are embers of health and restoration. To appreciate them and to make use of the hope that they offer, we must be open to accept a new brand of "experts" whose authority lies in their effectiveness rather than in professional accreditation or advanced academic degrees. In this, we can be guided by the biblical story of Joseph.[5]

Joseph was one of twelve sons of Israel (Jacob). His mother died as she gave birth, and Joseph became his father's best loved son. Joseph's brothers had always been envious of him, but when he related a dream in which they bowed in supplication to him, their anger ignited and they conspired to kill him.

One day, when they were far from home tending sheep, the brothers seized Joseph and threw him into a pit. While they were arguing about how to dispose of him, a caravan of Ishmaelites passed by on their way to Egypt. The brothers agreed to sell Joseph as a slave to these traders rather than killing him. To explain Joseph's disappearance, they took a cherished cloak that had been given to him by their father and soaked it in the blood of a sheep as evidence that Joseph had been attacked and killed by wild animals.

While Israel mourned his son, Joseph was sold in Egypt to the Pharaoh's personal assistant, Potiphar. Joseph embraced his fate and served faithfully and diligently in Potiphar's household. In return for his loyal service, Joseph was eventually appointed supervisor over all Potiphar's servants and became the chief administrator of his household.

In spite of his purity, Potiphar's wife began to lust for Joseph who was handsome and young. Joseph rejected her seductions, proclaiming, "My master trusts me with everything in the entire household. He has made me equal in authority and has held back nothing from me other than you, his wife. How could I do such a wicked thing as to violate his trust? It would be a great sin against God!"

In a desperate effort to get away, Joseph fled the house, leaving behind the cloak that his master's wife had torn from him. In retaliation for this rejection, Potiphar's wife claimed that Joseph had attempted to rape her and used the cloak as evidence against him. Joseph was apprehended and imprisoned.

Even in the depths of the dungeon, Joseph accepted his fate and served faithfully. He was, even in prison, again raised to a position of leadership and was placed in charge of the other prisoners. Two of the Pharaoh's servants who were also imprisoned at that time on charges of theft learned of Joseph's ability to interpret dreams and beseeched him to explain their dreams, promising that, in return, they would help him after they were released. On the basis of their dreams, Joseph correctly predicted that one of the servants, a cup-bearer, would be released and promoted and that the other, a baker, would be hanged.

The servant who was released soon forgot his promise to help, and Joseph remained in prison. It was only years later, when the Pharaoh himself was troubled by ominous dreams which none of his counselors or astrologers could interpret, that the servant told him of the Hebrew boy and his ability to decipher dreams. Joseph was cleaned up and summoned to the Pharaoh's court.

When the Pharaoh described his dreams, Joseph replied that they were portents that seven years of bountiful harvest would be followed by seven years of famine. He advised that, during the prosperous years, one-fifth of all that was produced should be stored in preparation for the famine and that an administrator should be appointed to oversee this effort.

The Pharaoh was not deterred by the fact that Joseph was not of the same background, that he came from a "dysfunctional Hebrew family," or that he was a prisoner. He trusted and followed Joseph's advice, and even appointed him to administer his harvest, awarding him power of office second only to his own.

When the famine came, the Pharaoh's was the only land that was prepared. The Bible recounts that Egypt not only survived the famine but prospered for four hundred years until "there arose a Pharaoh who knew not Joseph."

Today, in communities throughout the nation, hundreds of "modern-day Josephs" are at work, restoring spiritual health in their neighborhoods, guiding others to lives of value and fulfillment. Although Joseph was betrayed and treated unjustly, he always held firmly to the belief that God could work through any situation, and even in the worst circumstances he continued to serve without resentment. He never yielded to bitterness and his attitude determined his availability to God. Likewise, our modern-day "Josephs" have faced adversity and injustice without bitterness or resentment. Like Joseph, they are evidence that victims are not created by victimizers, but they become victims because of their own attitudes. A victimizer can injure or even kill, but it takes another's willing participation—and acceptance—to become a victim.

The answers to the problems America faces can be found in our own modern-day Josephs. Many of these community healers have come out of our prisons. They have experienced what it is to live in drug-infested, crime-ridden neighborhoods. Many have themselves fallen but have been able to recover through their faith in God. Their authority is attested to, not by their position and prestige in society, but by the thousands of lives they have been able to reach and change.

- In San Antonio, Texas, a recovered drug addict and his wife launched a ministry and have freed more than thirteen thousand drug abusers and alcoholics from their addictions.
- In Hartford, Connecticut, a man whose brother was paralyzed in an attack by a crazed youth dedicated his life to turning young people from violence. His tireless efforts won the trust of the leader of one of the most notorious gangs and, working together, the two have turned hundreds of young people from lives of violence and crime to positive, productive lives.
- In Atlanta, Georgia, one man made a commitment to salvage the lives of homeless addicts and now walks daily under the viaducts and through the back alleys of the city to seek out the people who need his help. Time and again, he has transformed desolate street people to productive, energetic citizens.

Our modern-day Josephs are working with individuals that all the conventional service deliverers have given up on. They embrace the worst cases and they work with meager resources, yet their effectiveness eclipses that of conventional professional remedies. One faith-based substance abuse program, for example, is able to effect its cures at a cost of only $50 per person, per day, yet has a 70 percent success rate, in stark contrast with conventional therapeutic programs for substance abusers that charge up to $600 a day per client and yet have only single-digit success rates.

Why haven't we heard more about these modern-day Josephs? Why isn't their success common knowledge? Why haven't we tapped their great potential to address not only the needs of the underclass but the problems that exist among every race, ethnicity, and income bracket?

The main reason that today's Josephs go unrecognized,

unappreciated, and underutilized is, simply put, elitism. Elitism has caused us to dismiss the possibility that remedies can emerge from the residents of low-income neighborhoods. There is a widely accepted portrait of the poor as hapless victims with few if any redeeming qualities, swimming in a sea of pathology and waiting for rescue from the outside by professional experts. We are confronted with this caricature of the poor in virtually every arena: academia, the news media, and entertainment television.

We have invested millions of dollars to hire researchers to conduct "failure studies" of the poor. These researchers take their notebooks into low-income communities and tally how many people are on drugs and in prison, how many young girls are pregnant, and how many youths have dropped out of school. They do not look for models of success—families that, in spite of similar circumstances, have raised children who have refused the lures of drugs and gangs, who have stayed in school, who have not had babies out of wedlock. They do not document the efforts of community activists in those same neighborhoods who have engendered literal transformations in lives that were being wasted by addictions and violence. Scholars on both the left and right make comfortable livings detailing the pathologies of the poor without ever talking with a single poor person.

Our news media also emphasize the dysfunction of low-income communities. Multiple murders and street violence sell newspapers. Salvaged lives do not. One friend who worked with young gang members in Hartford, Connecticut, told me that when the youths he worked with turned their lives around, the newspapers lost interest in their stories, and this had an effect on the young people. He described their experience:

> *On Halloween, the kids gave parties for the younger brothers;*
> *they gave senior citizens turkeys, needy families turkeys; they*
> *did a lot of positive things. But they found that they weren't*
> *getting the kind of recognition that they had when there were*
> *gang wars. Articles did not show up on the front page—but on*
> *the back page. . . . They could hardly find them, the articles*
> *were so small. But when they were fighting, they were on the*
> *front page.*

Not long ago, I was invited to appear in a television news series on racism hosted by Ted Koppel. Blacks were invited as victims of racism and economic disadvantage and were not expected or welcomed to suggest any solutions to the problems faced by their communities. Before we went on the air, we were coached to think of our best personal "lynching story." When I said that the greatest enemy of the black community is not on the outside and that personal responsibility and a belief in self-determination also have a critical impact on our condition, I was criticized for "mixing apples and oranges."

Television talk shows, such as *Sally Jessy Raphael* and *Ricki Lake,* have become virtual circuses in which the deformities and wounds of low-income people are continually put on display. The producers of these shows know that the more shocking the societal aberrations they present, the higher their ratings will be. So the American public is presented daily with a carnival show of moral deviance—youths who have committed violent crimes, men who have had sex with their girlfriends' daughters, and mothers who date their daughters' boyfriends. The lifeblood of such shows is conflict, despair, and bizarre values and the examples displayed are almost exclusively low-income and working-class people. Guests on these talk shows do not include the Terry McGoverns or

Margaux Hemingways of society. The only time we hear of deviance among upper-income people is when they have graduated from the Betty Ford clinic and are publicizing their books about their past experiences. The public is shown a sanitized version of the struggles of upper-income individuals, yet we are allowed to peer into the most lurid details of social dysfunction found among the poor. While low-income people are exposed on the *Jenny Jones Show*, their upper-income counterparts appear only for the objective discussion of the *Charlie Rose* show.

The media have played a major role in propagating the belief that solutions could never be found in our low-income communities, and that the experts on the poor are the non-poor. But the media are not the only agents of this deception: They take their cues from much larger and more powerful institutions.

There are many powerful social, economic, and political institutions that have a proprietary interest in continued existence of the problems of the poor, the denial of the existence of solutions, and the portrayal of low-income people as victims in need of defense and rescue. These powerful interest groups include members of the civil rights establishment, a massive poverty industry that owes its existence to the problems of the poor, and politicians who are aligned with them. They are the modern-day equivalents of the Pharaoh's court counselors who view our Joseph's ability to heal people and solve their problems as a threat to their own domain of "expertise."

"Experts," whose careers and celebrity status depend upon the existence of a problem, can write about the problem, consult about it, and speak about it on talk shows—they can do everything but solve the problem. These experts have a clear financial interest in perpetuating the problems of the poor. The poor represent a $340 billion commodity, in terms of annual allotments to federal and state programs that have been instituted in their name. The institutions with a vested interest in the continuance and expansion of this funding have formed a virtual iron triangle that has blocked the message that solutions to the most critical problems of the poor already exist and that they are to be found, not among the credentialed, professional experts, but in the neighborhoods that suffer the problems. The civil rights establishment, the poverty industry, and their political affiliates will not easily relinquish their position as custodians of the poor nor their "ownership" of the problems of poverty. Like conspirators in the Pharaoh's court, they have formed an alliance of mutual support and joint opposition to any unwelcome competition.

Chapter 2

Conspiracy in the Pharaoh's Court

J ust as the Pharaoh's embrace of Joseph may have been viewed with contempt and jealousy by the astrologers and magicians that he had previously consulted for guidance, modern-day Josephs also meet opposition from turf-guarding counselors of today's "pharaohs." As concern with power, prestige, and the purse have eclipsed concerns about solving the problems of the nation, a virtual conspiracy has taken shape in the pharaoh's court.

Among the conventional court counselors who have viewed the rise of Joseph as a threat are members of the civil rights establishment. For years, the predominance and power of this faction has increased in direct proportion to the guilt produced by conditions suffered by minorities, in particular, low-income blacks. While civil rights court counselors took on the mantle as champions of the poor, many of the race-based policies they have promoted have done little to improve the conditions of those who are most in need.

The success of modern-day Josephs in empowering the poor challenges the position of the civil rights establishment as the premier spokesmen for low-income minorities. Based on principles of self-determination and personal responsibilities, the strategies of today's Josephs have done more to improve the condition of the poor than did an agenda focused on racial grievances and race-preferential policies.

To be fair, many of those who have failed to support today's Josephs do not have bad intentions. The Pharaoh's cup-bearer recognized Joseph's qualities when they were imprisoned together but, after his release, he failed to tell the Pharaoh about Joseph and his powers. In the same way, today's Josephs often receive only token recognition but are never linked to our modern-day "pharaohs": leaders in the business community, philanthropies, and government who could provide tangible support for their work.

In Washington, D.C., for example, a safehouse for children in one of the District's most desolate and dangerous areas was established by a retired boxer who offers counseling, tutoring, and recreational activities in a makeshift storefront facility. The walls in that safehouse are covered with plaques and certificates of appreciation given by various public officials, but most of these awards have been discolored by the rains that have seeped through the many holes in the roof.

There are others in today's pharaoh's court who simply dutifully perform their functions, assuming that, somehow, they are working for the good of society. As they carry out their duties in the ranks of large bureaucracies of service providers, they do not have the perspective to take into account the real-world consequences of their activities and they fail to recognize that in many cases their functions are either ineffective or counterproductive.

Regardless of intent, the compliance of these court functionaries gives tacit consent to the conspirators who have undermined support for the Josephs of our day.

THE CIVIL RIGHTS AGENDA: WHO WINS? WHO LOSES?

As early as 1965, William Raspberry, then a young reporter, headlined his feature on the "other Washington" with the following proclamation: "Civil Rights Gains Bypassing Poorest Negroes." The article read, in part:

> *Civil rights progress, remarkable as it has been in recent years, has bypassed poor Negroes. In the North especially, most civil rights gains have benefitted the Negro middle class and left the disadvantaged masses largely unaffected. This is particularly true in Washington, where a majority of the population is Negro. . . .*
>
> *"When the District passes a law barring discrimination in the sale of housing, that's progress all right," says Roena Rand, chairman of Washington's Congress of Racial Equality. "But it doesn't mean a thing to the little guy who can't afford to buy a house in the first place." . . .*
>
> *The same is true of other civil rights gains, such as opening of top-level jobs and desegregation of posh restaurants. Negroes who weren't doing badly to begin with are doing even better, while those at the bottom stay there. The result is a growing sense of frustration and hopelessness on the part of the unskilled, unlettered, and jobless slum dwellers as they see themselves falling farther and farther behind both whites and middle-class Negroes.[1]*

In the 1960s, I had a number of personal experiences in which I saw that low-income blacks were often left behind.

The prizes won in battles fought by the poor often went to blacks who were not in poverty. In West Chester, Pennsylvania, I once led a demonstration against a pharmaceutical company that had a history of racial discrimination in its hiring practices. The foot soldiers in this demonstration were humble grassroots blacks—janitors, laborers, and hairdressers—who stood for days at the gates of the company with picket signs. When the company finally relented, it announced that it would hire nine blacks. As it turned out, all nine of the new employees held doctorates in chemistry. When we approached these black chemists asking them to support our efforts to open additional jobs at other levels in the company, they kept us at arm's length. They denied that their hiring was related to our efforts and informed us that they had been hired on the basis of their merit. Regardless of their degrees, I knew that, had there been no demonstration, those black chemists would not have been hired.

From its inception, the struggle for civil rights was fraught with certain moral inconsistencies that would limit its success. As early as the mid-1960s, the foundation on which the movement was built began to exhibit cracks, and warning lights were flashing regarding the potential for growing bifurcation within the black community. The needs of those who were suffering the most critical problems were overlooked as—for reasons that will be later discussed—leaders of the movement continued to pursue remedies that were based on racial preference rather than actual economic or social disadvantage. When opportunities for employment and education are offered on the basis of race alone, the main beneficiaries will be those who are best prepared to take advantage of those opportunities, not those who are most in need.

The split between the demands of the leaders of the civil rights establishment and the concerns of their purported constituents has widened throughout the last thirty years. On a number of issues that would primarily impact conditions in low-income communities, grassroots blacks have registered opinions that are sharply at odds with the positions taken by the civil rights cadres. In one survey sponsored by Home Box Office, Inc. and conducted by the Joint Center for Political and Economic studies, 83 percent of black respondents who knew about school vouchers said they were in favor of choice programs "where parents can send their children to any public or private school that will accept them."[2] Yet in a floor vote at the 1993 NAACP convention, delegates passed a resolution opposing voucher programs that would provide low-income children with the means to attend private schools. When *Washington Post* pollsters asked whether minorities should receive preferential treatment to make up for past discrimination, 77 percent of black leaders said yes, while 77 percent of the black public said no. In addition, a majority of the black populace disapproved of forced school busing, while 68 percent of black leaders supported busing.[3] Another survey of the black population taken by a research group, Fabrizio, McLaughlin, and Associates, in 1993 revealed that 91 percent of the respondents were in favor of requiring able-bodied welfare recipients to work for their benefits and 59 percent favored eliminating parole for repeat violent offenders. In a *Wall Street Journal*/NBC News poll, 47 percent of black respondents were *not* in favor of race-based affirmative action programs, an issue vehemently defended by the NAACP and the Urban League. In another *Wall Street Journal*/NBC News poll of September 1994, when asked to cite the issue of greatest importance to the black community, 54 percent of blacks polled said "increased economic opportunity" and 33 percent said "stronger black-run institutions," while only 8 percent replied "greater racial integration."[4] Yet the purported spokespersons of the black community, the civil rights leaders, continue to pursue their agenda of the sixties: mandated integration and recompense for past discrimination.

In light of a fundamental disagreement between the black leadership and populace on issues that are critical to the black community, it is small wonder that an organization such as the NAACP has lost at least 100,000 members during the past ten years.

In an important sense, the debate that surrounded the appointment of Clarence Thomas to the Supreme Court can be viewed as a nationwide referendum of blacks regarding the values and goals that should guide the black community. Clarence Thomas emphasized personal responsibility and self-help and he demanded equality of opportunity rather than guaranteed equality of results. This message resonated with grassroots blacks. Polls consistently revealed that the majority of the black populace supported Thomas's nomination and that the lower the income level, the greater the support. At the same time, Clarence Thomas's greatest antagonists were leaders of the civil rights establishment who viewed his positions as a threat to their agenda of race-based grievances.

Those whose careers or celebrity status rest on the premise that the greatest single obstacle to black achievement is racism have enforced a gag rule on others who say that self-help and personal responsibility are the keys to progress. This censorship has noteworthy precedents. At the turn of the century, Booker T. Washington warned against the agenda of those "problem profiteers," proclaiming:

> *There is a class of colored people who make a business of keep-*
> *ing the troubles, the wrongs, and the hardships of the Negro*
> *race before the public. Having learned that they are able to*
> *make a living out of their troubles, they have grown into the*
> *settled habit of advertising their wrongs—partly because they*
> *want sympathy, and partly because it pays. Some of these peo-*
> *ple do not want the Negro to lose his grievances, because they*
> *do not want to lose their jobs.[5]*

Through the years, the bait-and-switch game has continued in which the conditions of poor blacks have been used to justify policies and programs whose main beneficiaries were upper- and middle-income blacks. Consider the demands made by black "spokesmen" in 1990 regarding charges that inner-city youngsters were being exploited by the Nike Corporation, which was using advertisements to entice them to spend their meager resources on high-priced running shoes. Among the "solutions" to this situation which were posited by Jesse Jackson's organization PUSH were demands that a greater number of blacks be placed in top management positions at Nike, that more advertising be placed in media outlets owned by blacks, and that blacks be given more seats on the corporation's board. Struck by the ironic misfit of problem and solution, Bill Raspberry wrote, "The inner-city poor furnish the statistical base for the proposals, but the benefits go primarily to the already well-off. Black executives who already hold good jobs get promoted to better ones; blacks who already sit on important corporate boards get another directorship. And the people who provide the statistical base get nothing.[6]

Like PUSH's demands on Nike, race-preferential policies such as affirmative action are destined to promote the interests of middle- and upper-income blacks rather than the concerns of the poor. Simply put, programs of affirmative action, set-asides, and policies for racially "proportionate" hiring and academic admission will be of most benefit to minorities who are already equipped and prepared to take advantage of the opportunities they provide.

For example, in 1989, 14 percent of the "disadvantaged" black students who were admitted to the University of California at Berkeley came from households with annual incomes above $75,000.[7] Set-asides for minority businesses through the Small Business Administration's 8(a) program have, likewise, primarily enriched a relative handful of minority firms whose owners are not at all disadvantaged. According to the General Accounting Office, about 1 percent of the 5,155 firms in the 8(a) program received one-quarter of the $4.4 billion in contract dollars awarded in fiscal 1994.

In 1978, in order to deal with the problem of an underrepresentation of positive images of blacks in the entertainment media, the Federal Communications Commission established a program through which substantial tax breaks were given to corporations that sold television and radio rights to minorities. Once again, this policy was abused in a variation of a long-standing bait-and-switch game. An existing racial disparity was used to justify programs that brought benefits to a handful of upper-income blacks.

In numerous instances, blacks have served as "fronts" for white companies in exchange for a portion of the windfall profits that accrued from these sales. In 1995, one media giant, Viacom, Inc., was scheduled to receive a tax break of up to $640 million for selling its cable TV system for $2.3 billion to a consortium led by black investor Frank Washington, although Washington had only a $1 million stake in the deal and would be able to withdraw himself after only three years with a $2 million profit. Such deals were not foreign to Mr. Washington who, incidentally, had helped draft the legislation as an FCC lawyer. Washington had previously been involved in a number of other cable sales deals—one with the Hearst Corp. and three with Jack Kent Cooke.

And Mr. Washington was certainly not the only mogul to capitalize on the FCC program. Harvey Gantt, a black who was formerly the mayor of Charlotte, North Carolina, was challenged for similar dealings and defended his own behavior by declaring that he had done nothing "illegal." According to the Federal Communications Commission, of the 192 radio stations transferred to minority ownership under Section 1071 of the tax code since 1978, 130 were sold within a period averaging four years.[8]

While conditions of low-income blacks have been used in such bait-and-switch games to further an agenda based on racial grievances, poor blacks have also suffered from outright opportunism on the part of many of their purported spokespersons. In one sense, poor blacks are more victimized today by black-on-black greed, corruption, and incompetence than they are by racists. One notorious example of abuse of privilege is the case of former NAACP executive director, Ben Chavis, who authorized the payment of up to $332,400 out of the treasury of his financially strapped organization to pay a woman who was threatening him with a sexual discrimination lawsuit.[9] Chavis was not the first official of the NAACP to misuse the funds of the organization, even when it was millions of dollars in debt. Consider the following news item from July 14, 1995:

An audit released yesterday found that some NAACP officers squandered money on limousines, personal trips, and clothing at a time when the civil rights organization was plunging into debt. . . . The audit focuses primarily on three former NAACP officers—Benjamin L. Hooks, who was executive director for 15 years; the Rev. Benjamin F. Chavis, Jr., who replaced Mr. Hooks in 1993 and was dismissed last year after spending $300,000 in NAACP money to settle a sexual discrimination and harassment lawsuit; and Dr. William F. Gibson, longtime chairman of the 64-member board.[10]

In the early 1970s while I served as a program director for the Urban League, I felt the effects of similar opportunism. I realized that funds for one of my projects were being filtered to other uses when a $300,000 grant for at-risk youths was mysteriously depleted to $180,000. At that time, it was also taken as a given that many of the League's conferences would be scheduled to coincide with the dates and locations of Superbowl games. It also became the custom among many project directors to award lucrative contracts to "consulting firms" that had been set up by their family and friends, who often lacked the qualifications or expertise necessary to do the job.

During the Nixon administration, $30 million had been awarded to the National Urban League and more than $60 million to its affiliate organizations. An audit of the Urban League during the Ford administration revealed that numerous programs could produce no verifiable deliverables for the funds they had received.

Given the tilt that the civil rights agenda has had towards the interests of blacks who are best prepared, it is not surprising that from 1970 to 1976 black families with incomes over $35,000 grew from 17.7 to 21.2 percent of the black population and that those with incomes over $50,000 nearly doubled from 4.7 to 8.7 percent, while the percentage of black families with incomes less than $10,000 continued to grow.[11] In light of the careers, power, and paychecks that depend on retaining the thirty-year-old civil rights agenda, it is to be expected that the civil rights establishment would vehemently oppose any reform that would entail policies based on economic and social disadvantage rather than race. In fact, many leaders of the civil rights establishment have become players in a collaborative effort to block reform, and have contributed to the conspiracy to silence news of alternative solutions for the problems of blacks who are in poverty.

THE PHARAOH'S MAGICIANS AND THE POVERTY INDUSTRY

The second flank of court conspirators are members of what I call the poverty industry. A virtual twin of the civil rights movement, the poverty industry was conceived in the same womb in the mid-1960s, in an era of tragic racial disparity and discrimination. In 1964, the same year that the landmark Civil Rights Act was passed, a host of anti-poverty programs were also spawned, including food stamp legislation, the Economic Opportunity Act (which was the cornerstone of the War on Poverty), and programs for mass transportation. On the heels of this legislation, in 1965, additional legislation included Medicare and Medicaid, the Elementary and Secondary Education Act, the Higher Education Act, and the Public Works and Economic Development Act. Because of the close alignment—both in chronology and rationale—between the civil rights movement and the poverty industry, the moral authority of one has been extended to the other, and criticism of either—however well founded it may be—is considered blasphemy.

In essence, the poverty programs were advertised as the means of fulfilling the civil rights promise in a nation burdened by the guilt of a history of racial discrimination. However, like the misdirected civil rights agenda, the programs and policies of the poverty industry are embraced on the basis of their purported intent alone, without regard to their success or failure in achieving their purpose. Powerful economic interests which derive their legitimacy from the civil rights establishment have now calcified around old racial wounds.

As the poverty industry continued to mushroom, funds initially designated as cash benefits to the poor were channeled, instead, to bureaucracies of service providers. According to a number of studies, 70 cents of every dollar designated to relieve poverty is absorbed by the service professionals, while only 30 cents reaches the hand of a poor individual.[12] Between 1960 and 1985, noncash programs for services and commodities grew 1,760 percent. In 1985, cash income programs amounted to $32.3 billion, while commodity and service programs received $99.7 billion.[13] These service programs have congealed into a virtual poverty industry which has a vested interest, not in boosting the poor to self-sufficiency, but in maintaining and expanding a client base of dependents.

John McKnight, director of a community studies program at Northwestern University, describes the onslaught of professional caretakers in language that is poignant and poetic:

There are low-income neighborhoods where so many people live lives surrounded by services that the neighborhood itself be-

comes a forest. People who live in this neighborhood forest are now called the "underclass." This is an obvious misnomer. Instead, we should say that the neighborhood is a place where citizens act as anyone else would if their lives were similarly surrounded and controlled by paid service professionals. A more accurate label than "underclass" would be "dependent on human service systems." A more accurate differentiation of status would be to say the residents are "clients" rather than citizens.[14]

Ironically, while a disproportionate number of blacks are in poverty, a much greater percentage of blacks than whites are employed by the poverty industry where they function as the custodians of the poor. While only two out of ten college-educated whites now work for the government, as many as six out of ten blacks with college educations hold government jobs—the majority with the social service industry or with the education system. Because the careers of these service providers are ensured by a client base of the poor who are dependent on them, the self-sufficiency of low-income blacks poses a threat to their guardians in the poverty industry. A condition now exists where the interests of one group of blacks is in direct conflict with the interests of another.

Within the last thirty years, an income gap has steadily widened within the black community. While blacks with adequate preparation rose to middle- and upper-income brackets, others—especially urban youths—fell further behind. In 1964, black unemployment among sixteen-year-old black males was 25.9 percent. By 1980, fifteen years after the War on Poverty was launched, it had risen to 37.7 percent.[15] Although blacks have made great strides in entering white-collar jobs since the passage of civil rights legislation, 55 percent of the increase in black professional, management, and technical employment between 1960 and 1976 was in the public sector. Social welfare positions accounted for half of the public jobs.[16] As early as the 1960s, sociologist Kenneth Clark had correctly sized up the modus operandi of the poverty industry as he complained about the emergence of "welfare colonialism."

One of the "colonies" that has brought rich resources to the social service system is the foster care system. Although recordkeeping has been notoriously sloppy and it is not certain exactly how many children are in the system, estimates range from half a million to 600,000. In 1991, the system was awarded a servicing budget of $9.1 billion, in spite of the fact that the adoption placement rates of the public agencies are dismal—as low as 33 percent of the cases in which adoption was actively initiated. The fact is that children bring more funds to the system if they are kept in foster care rather than placed in permanent adoptive homes. Studies have shown that as much as 70 percent of the funds allotted for foster care nationwide is spent on overhead and salaries. It was reported, for example, that one agency received $24,000 a year for each child in its care, but spent less than $3.00 a day to feed and clothe each child. In one city, four agencies received a total of $6 million to place two thousand children during a one-year period, yet only ten children were placed.[17] Many children are held hostage to the system until they "age out" when they are eighteen years old.

The saga of an acquaintance, Irene Pernsley, provides vivid details of the trap of the foster care system. In 1965 Pernsley, a black social worker in the midst of a divorce, discovered that her young teenage daughter was pregnant. Neither Irene nor her daughter considered abortion to be an option and, in what both believed to be the best interest of the child, the baby boy was placed with a publicly supported agency for adoption. Irene and her daughter were assured that since the child was a healthy male infant, placement would be no problem.

As she picked up the pieces of her life, Mrs. Pernsley eventually rose in her profession to become commissioner of Philadelphia's Department of Public Welfare, the agency responsible for adoption and foster care. However, in 1983—eighteen years after Irene's grandson had entered the foster care system—a nightmare began for the Pernsley family.

A friend of Irene's who was employed as a social worker was filing case records of youths who had aged out of the system when she noticed a teenager with the last name of Pernsley. Curious, she asked Irene if she had any relatives in the foster care system. Initially, Irene replied that she did not. In her mind, her grandson had been adopted nearly twenty years ago. But then doubt began to gnaw at her, and Irene sought additional information about the case. Though the information Pernsley sought was controlled by an agency that received most of its funds from her department, the agency initially refused to divulge the youth's case history and complied only when the case was brought to public attention. The records revealed that the young man was, in fact, her grandson and she was heartbroken to learn that he had spent his entire childhood shifting between the households of strangers and institutions.

At the time, the incident received much press coverage, but this episode was unique only because it involved a prominent public official. Trapped within the custodianship of the welfare state, thousands of other silent victims are even now coming of age within the system. A lifetime spent drifting within the foster care system has sealed the fates of many children. Studies have revealed that as many as 70 percent of prison inmates have spent some time in the foster care system. In effect, the system is incubating tomorrow's criminals at the public's expense, in the name of "rescuing the children."

When confronted with their dismal records of successful placement, adoption agencies allege that their failure to place is due to a lack of acceptable adoptive families and, in particular, to a dearth of black families willing to adopt. This myth was shattered years ago. In 1981, a nationwide survey revealed that, although many agencies claim that black families are not willing to adopt children, black families informally adopt ten times more children than are placed through formal adoptive agencies. In the black community, the extended family has traditionally played a crucial function in child rearing. One study described the prevalence of the extended family in the black community as follows: "Families cut across household divisions and, in many instances, single households are only part of larger family structures.... Among blacks, households centered around consanguineal relatives have as much legitimacy as family units as do households centered around conjugal unions."[18] Robert Hill, a sociologist and former director of resources at the National Urban League, conducted a study of informal adoption among black families in the late 1970s and released the following findings:

> *About three million children, almost half of whom are black, currently live in households of relatives, while millions more reside with relatives for shorter periods of time as a means of providing low-cost day care services for working parents. . . . One*

of the key functions performed by the black extended family is the informal adoption and foster care of children by grandparents, aunts and uncles and other kin.[19]

The fact that such a substantial number of black families are willing to adopt with no compensation for their efforts debunks the myth that blacks are not likely to adopt even when their costs are subsidized. In fact, 37 percent of black families polled in an American Enterprise Institute survey conducted in 1981 said they were interested in taking in a foster child while 30 percent said they would be interested in legal adoption. In all, three million black families indicated that they would be interested in adopting black children.[20]

The success rates of a number of private agencies whose primary goal is the placement of children in permanent adoptive homes provides further evidence of these statistics. For example, a Detroit-based program called "Homes for Black Children," under the leadership of a determined woman, Sydney Duncan, set out to remove the barriers that many prospective black adoptive families faced. In contrast to conventional agencies that charge placement fees of $5,000 and above, Homes for Black Children did not charge a fee, and made use of the concept of black extended families by deliberately seeking out households with "aunts," "uncles," or "grandparent" figures. This agency also dramatically reduced the duration of "home studies" (the evaluation of prospective adoptive homes) from a national average of two years to just under six months and slashed through webs of red tape with simple innovations such as providing adopting families with facsimile birth certificates when originals could not be located. The result? In its first year of operation, Homes for Black Children successfully placed more children in stable, loving adoptive homes than Detroit's twelve other public and private adoption agencies combined.

Angered by the self-serving practices of the foster care branch of the poverty industry, I took my case to a number of newspapers and talk shows. My appearance on Oprah Winfrey's show prompted a letter from a black military couple who had tried unsuccessfully for years to adopt a child, in spite of the loving home they offered and a list of volunteer and community activities that would fill a page. The letter described in detail the grueling interrogation they encountered, including questions asking "if we get along with our families, how much we weigh, and what our fantasies are." The family had submitted to a rigorous and costly home study by a social service agency, but their application was held until that study was deemed "not current" and no longer valid, although, as the wife explained, the only changes in the household were an increase in income, a promotion for her husband, and the construction of a third bathroom. Frustrated and perplexed, they asked, "When there are qualified homes that identify themselves and want children, why are they turned away?"

The bureaucratic red tape involved in adoption is insulting and stifling to prospective adoptive parents and has, especially, limited adoptions to black families. In Los Angeles County, for example, the majority of children held in the foster care system are black, although only 9 percent of the county's overall population is black. In spite of the great need for black adoptive homes, according to an Urban League study, the screen-out rate for blacks seeking to adopt ranges between 90 percent and 99 percent.

In the case of Washington, D.C., abuses and incompetency within the foster care system were so prevalent that in 1995 a federal judge intervened in the District's troubled welfare system, declaring that even after four years of limited judicial supervision, the city was not properly caring for or protecting the abused and neglected children that had been entrusted to it. U.S. District Judge Thomas Hogan ordered the D.C. government to relinquish authority over a $53 million-a-year program that cares for approximately five thousand abused and abandoned children. In his critique of the foster care system Hogan aptly summed up a mind-set that is far too prevalent within the agencies of the poverty industry—"Instead of worrying about the children, mid-level managers and higher-ups seem to be concerned with preserving their place in a bureaucracy hostile to change so they can qualify for retirement benefits."[21]

While the majority of employees of social service agencies intend no malice, the poverty industry, by its very nature, is geared toward self-perpetuation and the continued custodianship of its clients rather than toward their self-sufficiency and independence. It is no wonder that, just as the expenditure of billions of dollars has not resulted in significant adoption placement rates, a thirty-year, $5 trillion-dollar investment in the poverty industry has not made a dent in the poverty rate of this nation. With the support of the civil rights establishment, the poverty industry has become the second formidable flank of conspirators in the Pharaoh's court. This cabal has, thus far, effectively blocked any efforts for reform of the system and has kept the dialogue focused on issues of racial disparities and animosities.

Each cohort of conspirators evolved from an action-point of the civil rights agenda of the 1960s: The civil rights establishment emerged from demands for integration and restitution for racial grievances; the poverty industry arose from an attempt to address economic disparities; and, finally, efforts to increase voter participation and political representation calcified into a third flank of opposition.

POLITICIANS IN THE COURT

As early as the 1960s, there were strong indications that the rise of black political figures would not necessarily promote the interests of the poor. As was the case with the gains of the civil rights establishment and the dominance of poverty programs, the achievements blacks have made in the political arena—as issues of racial grievances, poverty, and liberal politics have intertwined—have often accrued to middle-class blacks at the expense of the poor. Low-income people have been viewed not in terms of the value of their input regarding public policy and legislation but in terms of their value as props for grievances and demands for reparations.

In 1964, for example, inspired by a hope that they could have input in the policy formulation of the Democratic National Convention, grassroots blacks from Mississippi—hairdressers, bus drivers, and waiters—invested all they had and risked their jobs and even their lives to travel to Atlantic City in hopes of being seated as delegates. But the Democratic "party of compassion" did not extend a welcome. President Lyndon Johnson, fearing that seating a black delegation would cost him the entire Southern vote, ordered Hubert Humphrey to curtail the efforts of the Mississippi Freedom Democratic Party and to prevent the issue of its representation from coming to the floor.

In the end, a compromise was reached in which two black leaders handpicked by Democratic operatives were acknowledged as delegates at large, but the rest of the members of the Freedom delegation were only allowed as spectators at the convention and were denied voting powers. One of them, Victoria Gray Adams, explained the situation: "They thought, you know, 'Hey this is something, it's better than nothing.' But the fact of the matter was it was nothing." Another member of the delegation, Cleve Sellars, lamented "We had come too far, worked too hard, suffered too much to go up there and not get anything but a crust of bread." And Bob Moses, a math teacher who had participated in the effort, succinctly describes the lesson he learned from the experience:

> *What happened there in '64 symbolized the situation that we're in now. That is, the national Democratic Party and the political leadership of that time said, "Okay, there's room for these kinds of people"—professional people within our group who were asked to become part and actually did become a part of the Democratic Party. But on the other hand, they said, "There isn't room for these people—the grassroots people, the sharecroppers, the common workers, the day workers. There's room for them as recipients of largess, poverty programs and the like. But there isn't room for them as participants in power sharing.[22]*

This use of poor blacks only as props in a grievance-based agenda among their purported allies had plenty of precedents and it was a precursor of the future. In recent times, Senator "Ted" Kennedy, the "lion of Liberalism," had only four blacks among the 128-member staff of the Senate Judiciary Committee he chaired. Likewise, when the Budget Committee was first established by Edmund Muskie, it did not have a single black staffer.

History teaches us that "advocates" of the poor do not

always recognize the value of the insight of their constituents. In the early 1800s even though white abolitionists welcomed blacks to recount their suffering, they did not invite their input on policy or their vision for the future. For example, after witnessing Frederick Douglass's oratorical talent, the head of the Massachusetts Anti-Slavery Society, William Lloyd Garrison, invited him to make appearances telling of his experiences as a slave. When Douglas said that he wanted to go beyond a recitation of the wrongs he endured to discuss his hopes for the future, Garrison advised that he just stick to his story telling. Others told Douglas that they would take care of the philosophy and that his role should be limited to telling the facts.[23]

After the breakthroughs of the civil rights legislation of the 1960s, there was a burst of political involvement and success for black political candidates, but these political victories did little to improve conditions of poor blacks. In fact, as the loose cannons of the War on Poverty began to fire away in impoverished neighborhoods, many black elected officials were complicit in some projects that did more damage to black communities than even the previous onslaughts of the KKK and Night Riders were able to accomplish. Among these tragic ventures was one euphemistically dubbed "Urban Renewal," which uprooted many historical black neighborhoods to make way for public housing and other failed experiments of professional social engineers.

Throughout the first half of the century, black business districts had flourished in cities such as Tulsa, Oklahoma, and Durham, North Carolina. Tulsa's locus of black entrepreneurship was called "Deep Greenwood" and was known as the "Negro Wall Street." It was described by Scott Ellsworth in his book *Death in a Promised Land:*

> *Two- and three-story brick buildings lined the avenue, hous-*
> *ing a variety of commercial establishments including a dry-*
> *goods store, two theaters, grocery stores, confectioneries,*
> *restaurants and billiard halls. A number of black Tulsa's*
> *eleven rooming houses and four hotels were located here. "Deep*
> *Greenwood" was also a favorite place for the offices of Tulsa's*
> *unusually large number of black lawyers, doctors, and other*
> *professionals.*[24]

Similarly, the black business district of Durham, dubbed
"Hayti," was a mecca of entrepreneurship. By 1945 it was
home to hundreds of businesses from appliance stores and
laundromats to movie theaters and restaurants and was the
locale of a number of significant fraternal organizations.

With pure determination and strong networks of mutual
financial support, the businesses had survived the harrows of
the Great Depression. Greenwood entrepreneurs even exhibited the resolve necessary to rebuild their district after ri-
oting whites burned more than eight hundred businesses
and homes in 1921. But that bootstrap resilience was no
match for the powerful bulldozers of urban renewal which
sealed the fate of the Old Hayti section.

With full cooperation of black elected officials, plans were
made to build a new interstate highway system directly
through the business district. In the name of progress and renewal, more than six hundred families and one hundred
businesses were displaced and some seventy acres were
razed. Displaced residents of the once solid community were
scattered helter-skelter along long arterial stretches, and
black consumers had to travel by car even to make small pur-
chases. White-owned shopping malls and chain operations
began to reap the benefits of the black dollar that had once

circulated five and six times within the Old Hayti community. One black entrepreneur, Nathaniel White, recalled the site of the "renewal": "It was as if a bomb had been dropped on the neighborhood." Another resident of Durham lamented, "The whole sorry affair was done by design; we were misled by black politicians who fooled the majority of voters into thinking urban renewal would be good for them."

Today, black mayors are at the helm of many of our nation's largest cities, and more than eight thousand blacks hold elected offices throughout the country. Yet poor blacks are no better off in many cities under black stewardship than they were when their cities were run by whites.

Consider, for example, the city of Washington, D.C. The District of Columbia has been under black leadership for twenty years, with blacks holding the positions of mayor, police officers, superintendent of schools, and most of the city council seats. According to 1995 statistics, the District has the highest per-capita murder and violent crime rates in the nation, the highest percentage of residents on public assistance, and the lowest SAT scores—yet the highest paid school board.[25] Its neighborhoods, once stable and thriving with activity, have been reduced to economic wastelands where law-abiding residents live in fear. Because of incompetence and/or corruption in management practices, a number of the District's social service agencies and institutions have been placed in receivership. The *Washington Post*'s Colbert King gives the following comments on the state of the District:

A case in point is the tragic situation at D.C. Village, where some of the city's elderly and mentally retarded are housed. The Justice Department calls the situation "dangerous." Thirty-

seven needless deaths and bedridden residents losing limbs to bedsores and squalid conditions brought on by shoddy and insensitive staff work helped the Justice Department reach that conclusion. . . . The city's entire public housing agency, judged among the nation's worst, is in the hands of a court-appointed receiver . . . [and] a court-appointed receiver will soon take custody of the city's troubled foster-care program. . . . Then there is the Corrections Department, an agency in a class by itself, . . . operating under 11 different court orders . . . and looking at a request for the appointment of a receiver to take over the D.C. Jail's medical and mental health system.[26]

Washington, D.C., provides a case study of the intertwining confluence of interest that exists between the political and social service flanks of the Pharaoh's counselors. In May 1995, a public disclosure regarding conditions at the D.C. morgue sent shock waves through a horrified public. It was revealed that, because the morgue's crematorium was broken, seventy-four corpses—more than three times the morgue's intended capacity—were being stored in the facility where refrigeration has repeatedly been cut off during heavy rains. The morgue was not even supplied with an adequate number of body bags, cockroaches crawled across autopsy tables, and because of clogged drains, blood and body fluids backed up onto the floor. Conditions at the morgue hampered the efforts of law enforcement officials who have not had functioning equipment, for example, to determine whether children have died of sudden infant death syndrome or were the victims of suffocation. City officials have declared that, because the air conditioning was not functioning and because ventilation was so bad, the fetid air posed dangers to the employees' health.[27]

Now, no great clamor has been raised by middle-class blacks, or by leaders of child welfare organizations about the bodies of children in the morgue whose cause of death remains undetermined. Blacks in the upper- and middle-income brackets do not have deceased relatives lying in the fetid conditions of the morgue. They are not employed as staff of that decrepit facility, nor do they have relatives trapped in the no-man's-land of the city's facility for the elderly. With regard to the suffering inflicted on blacks by the greed or incompetence of other blacks, the civil rights establishment has remained silent.

Just a day after conditions at the D.C. morgue were brought to public attention, it was revealed that Washington's mental health facilities were in a state of chaos. One black-owned company, JMC, which had been hired to shelter and treat the city's mentally ill and received $4 million a year, was placed under an investigation to determine just how those funds were used. It was revealed that the company failed to provide proper therapy, social work, and housing for men and women with severe psychiatric disorders and that residents of its facilities had to buy their own food and scavenge the closets of a local psychiatric hospital for such basic necessities as toilet paper. Yet, as the quality of JMC's services and finances were deteriorating, the company was receiving preferential treatment from the District. Department of Human Service officials overrode the city's financial management system and issued handwritten checks to the company for more than $250,000. JMC received those checks, incidentally, shortly after it had hired John Clyburn as its chief executive officer. Clyburn, a longtime friend of D.C. Mayor Marion Barry, held large city contracts in the mid-1980s. In 1990, he and former District human service director David Rivers, who now rents a house to JMC for $1,100 a month, were tried and acquitted on federal bribery and conspiracy charges stemming from accusations that they had steered more than a dozen Human Service contracts worth $2 million to companies owned by Clyburn and his friends, one of which was JMC.[28]

Clearly, racially representative leadership alone does not ensure that conditions of low-income blacks will improve. While such corrupt and self-serving practices within the social service industry and the political arena have taken a tragic toll on blacks who are held in the trap of poverty, those who have tried to achieve economic self-sufficiency through small businesses have often found themselves hamstrung by regulations and restrictions which were instituted decades ago with racist intent but are now being enforced by black elected officials.

In Washington, D.C., for example, a decades-old law that prohibited "bootblacks" from the District was used against a black entrepreneur who had set up a thriving business of shoe-shine stands throughout the city, staffed by bow-tied employees, many of whom had formerly been unemployed. In another case, a hair salon whose practice was limited to braiding hair was threatened with termination because city regulations ruled that its stylists had to pass the same cosmetology exams as beauticians who use chemical treatments. As this entanglement with red tape shows, it is not the race of the ruler but the rules of the game that determine who wins and who loses.

As is the case with local-level political victories, the advance of black elected officials on the national level does not necessarily translate into victories for grassroots blacks. On the average, more than half the campaign funds of black congressional candidates come from labor unions and social service unions. Time and again, when grassroots blacks have been at odds with the unions on issues that impact their neighborhoods, the Congressional Black Caucus has come down on the side of the unions. Such is the case whenever the Davis-Bacon bill is brought into question.

The Davis-Bacon bill was introduced in 1931 by a New York congressman, Robert Bacon, who was angered because an Alabama contractor had successfully bid to build a federal hospital in his Long Island district. He had complained in a Labor Committee hearing that the largely minority work force brought in by the contractor had "entirely upset" local labor conditions. Bacon proposed a bill which would require all private contractors on federally funded projects to pay "prevailing" (union) wages. The bill was enthusiastically endorsed by organized labor, and the president of the American Federation of Labor, William Green, noted that "colored labor was being brought in to demoralize wage rates."

House debate lasted only forty minutes before the Davis-Bacon bill was approved. The racist motivation behind it was evident in remarks from Alabama Congressman Miles Allgood who apologized about the "bootleg labor" from his state and commented, "That contractor has cheap colored labor . . . and it is labor of that sort that is in competition with white labor. . . . It is very important that we enact this measure."

The Davis-Bacon bill worked as it was intended to. The year after it passed, only 30 of the 4,100 workers employed on the Boulder Dam project were black. Today, its effect is still the same, and it is felt most in inner cities where public-housing dollars are concentrated. The effect of the high wages that are mandated through the bill is to eliminate lesser-skilled laborers from competition for construction jobs in their neighborhood. Unemployed residents of public housing who would willingly perform painting and carpentry tasks sit idle as union workers earn top-dollar wages to reno-vate their properties.

Although it has been estimated that as many as 750,000 jobs could be opened to low-income laborers if the Davis-Bacon law were repealed, Black Caucus members, ever faith-ful to the labor unions, have been the most vehement opponents of any efforts to repeal it.

In similar fashion, black leaders with ties to unions moved to block a proposal by Indianapolis mayor, Steve Goldsmith, who sought to create jobs for low-income residents of his city by privatizing public transportation routes and utilizing shuttle services. And, in a similar move, in spite of over-whelming grassroots support for school vouchers which would enable low-income parents to send their children to the school of their choice, the Black Caucus has continually sided, not with its constituents, but with the teachers' unions and the public educational establishment to block school vouchers.

Members of the Caucus are also friends of the unions af-filiated with the public housing authorities (PHAs) which have been entrusted with billion-dollar budgets for the man-agement of housing projects. Like other arms of the poverty industry, the public housing conglomerate has profitably cashed in on the bait-and-switch game. Here, once again, conditions of the poor—predominantly, poor blacks—are used to justify funding flows that have never reached their communities. Black politicians have looked the other way as this game is played, and in cases where union interests are clearly at odds with the interests of their low-income con-stituents, they have sided with the unions.

In 1990, the federal government budget for modernization of public housing developments totaled $2 billion. In addition, $1.8 billion in federal funds were used to subsidize PHA operations in that year. Because of the massive budgets garnered in their name, public housing properties have become cash cows for unionized construction companies that have secured contracts to "rehab" public housing units. Investigations have shown that sloppy recordkeeping, corrupt contract practices, and construction invoices padded with charges for unauthorized additional work orders often characterized the management practices of the PHAs.

One investigation by the Housing and Urban Development's office of the inspector general included a multiregion review of Comprehensive Improvement Assistance Program (CIAP) funds which revealed that 82 percent of the PHAs that were audited "engaged in varying degrees of noncompliance with contract administration requirements." The same investigation found that 35 percent of the public housing authorities reviewed "charged ineligible and unsupported costs totalling $4.6 million to CIAP accounts" and that 64 percent "awarded approximately $4.2 million without obtaining the required bids or proposal."[29] The Elizabeth (New Jersey) Housing Authority, for example, awarded a $1,704,008 contract following noncompetitive procurement procedures suitable only for contracts under $10,000. A subsequent report issued by HUD found that the Elizabeth Housing Authority paid excessive salaries to high-level managers, placed relatives of housing authority commissioners in high-paying administrative positions, and procured consultant services without a contract, contrary to HUD requirements.[30]

In Philadelphia, the PHA's operating subsidy jumped 23 percent from $63,401,197 in 1989 to $78,288,008 in 1990 while the number of vacant units increased by 162. Housing authorities in Cleveland, New Orleans, and other cities exhibited similar trends over the same period.[31] In addition, PHAs have squandered millions of dollars by authorizing contract amendments—"change orders"—that may not have been necessary. The inspector general found that 42 percent of the PHAs it reviewed authorized change orders without obtaining necessary HUD approval or without "substantiating need for increased cost," racking up a total of $4.1 million unsupported or ineligible expenditures on change orders.[32] The St. Louis Housing Authority, for example, authorized fifty-nine change orders for one contractor that increased the costs of modernization by $935,626, without requisite competitive bidding for this work.

In spite of the multibillion dollars designated for public and assisted housing throughout the nation, public housing projects are notorious for their devastated, unlivable conditions. In addition, funds have been drained through incompetent and corrupt management practices and bloated bureaucracies have wasted and misused housing appropriations. A study of the housing authorities that have been designated as "most troubled" revealed that their administrative staffs exceeded HUD recommendations in amounts ranging from 143 percent to 271 percent.[33]

In the early 1980s, my organization, the National Center for Neighborhood Enterprise, was contacted by several groups of public housing residents throughout the nation who had joined together as volunteers to salvage their neighborhoods and were challenging the public housing authorities for the right to manage the properties in which they lived.

In the Bromley-Heath housing development in Boston,

residents revitalized a community recreation facility and established a baby sitting service, a radio station, and a volunteer tenant security patrol. In the Cochran Gardens project of St. Louis, residents rose to action when corpses were found in their elevators. The top four floors of their twelve-story high-rise—some 250 units—had been uninhabitable for more than a dozen years, and crime, vandalism, and drug-related murders filled the community with terror. The turnaround the residents accomplished when they were allowed to take on management duties won national acclaim, and their leader, Bertha Gilkey, was featured on CBS's *60 Minutes*. Sitting on a park bench in a landscaped courtyard, she reminded her interviewer that two years earlier he couldn't even have walked through that courtyard without the risk of being shot.

In Washington, D.C., the Kenilworth-Parkside public housing development stands out as a dynamic example of what can be accomplished when layers of bureaucracy are removed and real community control is achieved. During the 1960s and 1970s, under PHA management, Kenilworth-Parkside had been a classic example of a public housing program gone awry. The community was plagued with violent crime and drug trafficking and was rife with welfare dependency, teen pregnancy, and high school dropouts. Kimi Gray, the leader of the residents in this development who organized to take on their properties' management duties recalls, "In 1983, housing authority leadership was uniformly opposed to any type of resident involvement. Although our development had no heat or hot water, Kenilworth-Parkside was always classified as a low priority for modernization."

When residents finally won management duties, they addressed the needs of the community as a whole, establishing security patrols to oust drug dealers and launching a college preparation program, "College Here We Come," through which nearly six hundred youths from the development were placed in college within a twelve-year period. Within four years of resident management, welfare dependency was reduced by 50 percent, crime fell by 75 percent, and the rental receipts increased by 77 percent. A cost-benefit analysis conducted by an accounting firm projected that cost-efficient management by the residents would save the District government $4.5 million over a ten-year period.

The accomplishments of the residents at Kenilworth-Parkside were hard won. At one point, drug dealers who were angered about being evicted from their trafficking turf sabotaged the van that Gray used to transport her young students to their colleges, slashing the tires and filling the gas tank with dirt. But the residents prevailed, setting up substance abuse centers, youth counseling, a day-care center, and an on-site medical clinic. Their next hope was to go for the American Dream—to launch a home-ownership project that would offer residents the opportunity to hold assets that could give them upward mobility.

It might be expected that the political representatives of these low-income communities would applaud and support the victories achieved by their residents. But resident success proved to be unwanted competition for the housing authorities and their afffiliated unions, and many members of the Congressional Black Caucus chose to protect their bankrolls.

When one independent-minded member of the Caucus, then-Congressman Mike Espy, spoke in favor of the residents' home-ownership initiative, he was literally booed on the House floor by his colleagues. Representative William Clay (D-MO) dismissed the resident-empowerment proposal as a "hoax" and declared that he was "sick and tired of hearing about the wonderful accomplishments achieved at the Kenilworth Project." Likewise, Representative Maxine Waters (D-CA) called the proposal "ridiculous" and announced that she, too, was "sick and tired of them talking about what they are going to do once they are able to own a unit in Cabrini Green, or Carr Square, or in Nickerson Gardens"—all housing developments where the residents have pursued management responsibilities or ownership.

Resident leader Kimi Gray was incensed and explained, "Under resident management, we reduced crime, welfare dependency, recidivism, teen-age pregnancy, vandalism. We increased rent collections and set up businesses that employed residents. As the residents became confident in their ability to improve living conditions, they began seeking a more permanent stake in the future of the community. Homeownership may have been what the Administration wants to do, but it was our dream also. Nobody talks about that." The plight of the Kenilworth residents provides vivid evidence of the collision of the interests of low-income blacks and the interests of the Pharaoh's advisers who have built an empire on the deficiencies of the poor.

The "court counselors" have claimed ownership of the problems of the poor—in particular, poor blacks. As owners and experts on the problem, they can do a lot of things: they can write books about the problems, establish careers in the name of the problem, win office because of the problem, and appear on talk shows lamenting the problem. The only thing they cannot do is solve the problem.

In spite of the disastrous impact their agenda has had on their low-income constituents, black elected officials—like the civil rights establishment and representatives of the poverty industry—have been able to escape accountability through the same claim: "Racism is responsible for the conditions of the poor." They feel no obligation or responsibility to take part in the design of a solution. For these court counselors, the charge of "racism" serves as an escape clause in the informal contracts that exist between the leadership and their low-income constituents. In the same way, the civil rights legacy of the 1960s serves as a heat shield of moral authority that insulates them from any criticism of their agenda.

Chapter 3

A History Suppressed by the Pharaoh's Advisers

As the income gap within the black community steadily widens and low-income communities have been reduced to virtual war zones, the question emerges: If racial discrimination is the single culprit that produces black dysfunction, why aren't all blacks suffering equally? The failure to address that question has resulted in an era of opportunism by the spokespersons for an aggrieved race. We are now at a point where the champions of the black community are those who whine the loudest, whose complaints are the most persistent, and whose claims are the most outrageous—those who "rattle their cups the loudest."

The Guardians of Grievance, the cohort of advisers that are today's version of W. E. B. Du Bois' "talented tenth," have received support from black academicians and writers such as Cornel West. The writings of many of today's black scholars have amounted to no less than a revisionist history of the black community. This revised history focuses almost exclusively on the degradation whites have imposed on blacks and the accomplishments of the civil rights leadership's efforts since the sixties. Conveniently airbrushed from the portrait of black America are the remarkable models of self-help—accomplishments of black entrepreneurs and mutual aid societies even during eras of the most brutal racial repression and slavery. Lost is the legacy of personal responsibility and principle-based entrepreneurship that could provide today's youths with a pride in their heritage and an adaptable model that could guide their futures.

The selective history that is transmitted to our young people is, simply put, that blacks came to this country on slave ships; from there they went to the plantations and slavery, from the plantations to the ghetto, and, finally, to welfare. That's a simplified version of revisionist black history.

When students are taught black history, they read about the degradation and disadvantage their race has endured. When they seek black heroes, they are directed to Africa—Ancient Africa—for models. Dashikis have become the uniform of black studies departments and the donning of the kente cloth has become an intellectual rite of passage. These are emblems of status that is easily achieved. You don't need to accomplish anything. All you have to do is give evidence of your allegiance to cultural Afrocentrism.

Afrocentrism has become a major source of denial of responsibility. There is no call to responsibility as long as role models are limited to Ancient Africa, providing no personal challenge to act. There is little in Ancient Africa that young people can get their arms around and begin immediately to apply to their current environment. If black role models are mentioned, discussion is limited to such figures as Frederick

Douglass, Sojourner Truth, and Harriet Tubman—all of whom are compatible with a version of history that dwells on past grievances.

This is not in any way to denigrate the great accomplishments of those who challenged and defied the institution of slavery. But the history of the black struggle in America is incomplete unless it includes the stories of those who achieved economic and educational victories in the face of opposition and oppression, and in spite of slavery and the Jim Crow laws. For the last thirty years, there has been a virtual gag rule on the stories of these black heroes who could truly serve as role models for our young people.

Recently, when a newscaster interviewed a young black male and asked why he wasn't working, he replied that most of the available jobs were an hour away and he considered that too far to travel. In 1989, during the Miami riots, a television interviewer spoke with a local black "leader" and asked why American blacks had failed to pool their resources and launch small enterprises as other ethnic groups do. His response was that "piddling" little mom-and-pop stores were beneath the dignity of blacks.

The attitudes of these men are evidence that the lifeline has been severed between today's generation and the rich heritage of self-determination and the will to achieve that once provided a foundation for black progress, even against the greatest odds. A complete black history would reveal that, even in the face of the most bitter oppression and bondage, many courageous blacks persevered and accomplished, undaunted by the obstacles they faced.

The silenced black history includes the story of two slaves, Tony and Primus, who were bricklayers. Though they spent their days building a church under the supervision of their master, they secretly hired themselves out to local builders at night and on Sundays. Tony and Primus were not alone. Many other slaves who worked all day in the fields stole away under the cover of darkness at night to work for wages and then returned to the field in the morning for the next day's work. Money earned in this way was often used by slaves to purchase their freedom or the freedom of a friend or relative.

In spite of an era of unjust and despicable bondage, entrepreneurs also included female slaves who managed small businesses as seamstresses, laundresses, and weavers. Among these was a woman who received permission from her master to work for herself after her husband was sold. She set up two businesses—a coffee shop at an army garrison and a second-hand store that sold clothing and shoes.[1]

This resilient entrepreneurial spirit and belief in self-determination was acknowledged by syndicated columnist Walter Williams, who wrote:

> Sometimes whites didn't play fair in business, but whining was out and acumen in. Take Robert Gordon, who purchased his freedom and moved to Cincinnati, where he invested $15,000 in a coal yard and a private dock on the waterfront. White competitors tried to run him out of business through ruthless price cutting. Gordon simply hired fair-complexioned mulattoes to purchase coal from price-cutting competitors to fill his own customers' orders.[2]

In the past, a decline in racial animosity among whites was never considered a prerequisite for black progress. The most successful blacks did not spend a lot of time focusing on how they could change the attitude or actions of whites. For example, in 1863, white dock workers who were angry because blacks were being hired at Baltimore's shipyards called a strike that resulted in the dismissal of thousands of black workers. The black ship caulkers who had lost their jobs did not picket or stage demonstrations to vent their grievances. Instead they pooled their resources and formed their own cooperative business, the Chesapeake and Marine Railroad and Dry Dock Company, which operated successfully for eighteen years.

Tragically, although our current generation is presented with opportunities that our forebears never dreamed of, it is enslaved in ways that our ancestors never were. Today's youths have been indoctrinated with an ideology that has convinced them that their shortcomings are solely the result of racist oppression which has circumscribed their potential and has necessarily resulted in the rage, violence, and self-destruction that dominate their lives.

The bondage of that hopelessness and dependency could be broken by giving voice to the black heritage that was marked by determination, self-sufficiency and achievement. The truth is that values such as strong families, religion, patriotism, and self-reliance are deeply rooted in authentic black history.

At the eve of the Civil War, the combined assets of enterprising blacks totaled $50 million—in 1860 currency. Most of the enterprises launched by free blacks were in the service trades. Black entrepreneurs included barbers, hackmen, blacksmiths, grocers, tailors, restaurateurs, caterers, carpenters, and shoemakers.

The four pillars that provided a foundation for a stable black community, even during times of bitter racial animosity, were mutual assistance, strong moral principles, a commitment to educating the young, and a vibrant entrepreneurial spirit. As early as the 1700s, these values were embodied and sustained through two primary institutions of the black community which were closely interrelated—the church and fraternal or mutual benefit organizations. In the late eighteenth century, leaders urged blacks to avoid reliance on charity and promoted mutual aid organizations which they believed would encourage thrift, industry, and morality. The Free African Society, the first recorded black mutual aid organization, was founded in Philadelphia by Absolom Jones and Richard Allen in 1787. Members contributed one shilling a month to care for the needy with the stipulation that "their necessity was not brought by their own imprudence." Membership in the organization was denied anyone who was unwilling to live "an orderly and sober life."

By the 1830s, there were one hundred such organizations in Philadelphia alone, averaging 75 members each. In Baltimore, the southern city with the greatest number of benevolent societies, there were more than thirty associations, with membership tallies ranging from 35 to 150. Education and learning was highly valued and promoted. The Philadelphia Library Company of Colored Persons, for example, furnished a reading room with several hundred volumes and scheduled public debates on moral and literary topics. Through the combined efforts of the black churches and mutual benefit societies, free blacks established their own schools. By the beginning of the nineteenth century, two black schools had been established in Baltimore, and adults were pursuing the long-held dream of an education, studying Latin and French at night. In Washington, the first school for blacks was established in 1807 by three illiterate black men who constructed a small frame schoolhouse and hired a white teacher to instruct the children.

A concerted black effort against slavery was coordinated by the Negro Convention Movement which was launched in 1830, but the Convention focused on attitudes and actions within the black community as well. In addition to addressing racial prejudice, members of the Convention promoted the attainment of "the standard of a good society"—temperance, industry, thrift, and education. The Convention urged blacks to stress the importance of schooling, good moral character, and economic accumulation.

After the Civil War and the Emancipation, this same determination and will to achieve inspired remarkable economic and educational achievements among blacks who were just emerging from an era of oppression and slavery. Black progress in the thirty years following slavery surpassed achievements in the thirty years following the civil rights victories of the 1960s. The per-capita income of blacks skyrocketed by 300 percent during the first half century of freedom.[3] The American Missionary Association and other organizations established hundreds of schools serving tens of thousands of black students. As a result of such efforts, between 1865 and 1892, the rate of black illiteracy fell from 80 to 45 percent.[4] During the same period, as a result of the emphasis on education, the number of black newspapers increased from two to 154; attorneys from two to 250; and physicians from three to 749.[5]

When blacks were excluded from participation in the larger market economy, they established their own banks and insurance companies. At the turn of the century, for example, John Merrick, a black entrepreneur, established the North Carolina Mutual Life Insurance Company in Durham.

When the fledgling business's first claim of $40 came due, there was so little in the treasury that the officers contributed their own money to pay it. By 1939, however, the company employed more than a thousand people and served more than a quarter of a million policy holders. Other successful black businessmen include Henry Allen Boyd, the son of a slave with little education who established numerous businesses in Nashville, Tennessee, and supported the entrepreneurial efforts of other blacks; John Whitelaw Lewis who, when confronted with Washington's Jim Crow laws in 1913, established an elegant black hotel, which was designed by a black architect, built by black tradesmen, and became renowned as the center of social life for black professionals; and George Downing who established catering businesses in several eastern resorts in the 1840s and also built the luxurious Sea Girt Hotel in Newport, Rhode Island.[6]

Neither the 1896 *Plessy* v. *Ferguson* decision (which approved "separate but equal" segregated facilities) nor the Jim Crow laws (which were passed to eliminate black entrepreneurs and professionals from market competition) could stem the tide of successful black entrepreneurs. Between 1867 and 1917, the number of black enterprises increased from four thousand to fifty thousand.[7] In 1900, the National Negro Business League was organized by Booker T. Washington to encourage the further development of black businesses.

THE MESSAGE OF VICTIMIZATION

Tragically, today most of the loudest voices among black leaders make no mention of this rich black entrepreneurial legacy. Statistics about the differences between white incomes and black incomes are used to make the case of what white people must do, and it is presumed that blacks can advance only if and when whites change. Those same statistics could be used as a benchmark, a target which blacks ought to strive to achieve. In fact, that has been our approach when we met challenges in the athletic arena.

Although blacks had been shut out from professional sports, we asked only that the restrictions be removed and that we be given an opportunity to compete. Once allowed to participate in open competition, black athletes not only met previous standards but set new records. We are disproportionately successful in the arena of sports because we have practiced and pursued excellence. If we do not believe, as some racists do—or as sportscasters such as Jimmy the Greek or Al Campanis have been criticized for saying—that black athletic achievement is due to genetic traits and "breeding," we must recognize that our young men and young women have practiced to perfection. Yet we fail to admit that we can also achieve excellence by exhibiting the same diligence and effort in intellectual pursuits.

It is inconsistent that we ask only for the opportunity to compete on the basketball court or the football field, yet when we enter the computer lab and English department, we demand that the standards be lowered and that test scores be "race-normed." In spite of a history of being shut out of sports, we would be insulted by the suggestion that blacks coming up to bat be given four strikes before they're out. Nor would we demand that a black ballplayer's single should count as a double because of past discrimination or that a black player who is fouled should get three free throws instead of two. Yet this is the equivalent of what we demand when it comes to academic pursuits.

Black advocates of race-preferential policies who are whining about the barriers that we face in intellectual pursuits are demeaning their race, yet calling themselves "progressives." In March 1995, the president of Rutgers University, Francis Lawrence, started a bitter controversy when he commented that SAT testing was unfair to black students because they did not have the "genetic hereditary background" to achieve high scores. With these words, this liberal white academician, who had advocated affirmative action in admission policies and race-norming of grades, laid bare the tacit assumption that underlies such race-based preferential programs: the premise that racial differences, in and of themselves, can be equated with differences in capacity.

Professor Lawrence's slip of the tongue reveals the tragic turn the civil rights establishment made when it departed from demands for a level playing field and demanded instead a guaranteed percentage of the trophies. In justifying claims for preference "by virtue of victimization," civil rights leaders entered into a Faustian deal, trading a longstanding tradition of personal responsibility and self-sufficiency for a bevy of race-based entitlements. To claim that being black is a handicap for which compensation must be made is nothing short of a civil-rights inspired version of white supremacy.

Young people have much more to gain from studying models of achievement in the past than they do from hearing litanies of the wrongs that have been done to their people. They have more to gain from examples of excellence than from the chorus that sings "I've been 'buked and scorned."

Today's young people could gain inspiration from the story of the Golden Thirteen, a group of black navy men who served in World War II. In 1944, like other branches of the military, the U.S. Navy was segregated and black servicemen were relegated to such jobs as cooks and stewards. At the urging of Eleanor Roosevelt, President Franklin Roosevelt took measures to alleviate this racial discrimination and selected a number of blacks to attend a naval officer candidates school.

The small group of blacks who entered this training started with a setback. They were isolated and given only eight weeks to complete what was normally a sixteen-week session of training. Time was precious, and they wasted none of it complaining or staging protests. Instead, they formed an alliance of mutual cooperation and intense effort. When the nightly "lights out" order came, they covered their windows with blankets and studied through the night. They tutored and tested one another.

When their tests were graded at the end of the course, the marks of the Golden Thirteen were so high that the naval officers were suspicious and ordered them to be retested. The second time, their grades were even higher, averaging 3.89 out of a possible 4.0. The thirteen were awarded their commissions as ensigns on March 17, 1944 and were featured in *Life* magazine.

Clearly, the discrimination and disadvantage that these servicemen faced are to be abhorred and regretted, but who would not be inspired by their noble response—and their victory? In numerous more recent incidents, black youths who were labeled "at-risk" and thought of as teetering on the brink of failure have shown their ability to meet and surpass the highest academic standards when they were surrounded by encouragement and the expectation of success.

An account of the "Challenge" program for disadvantaged students at Georgia Tech, for example, gives strong evidence that expectations play an important role in performance.

When the Challenge course was initially presented as a remedial program to give less successful students a boost, a review of the program revealed that the kids who had enrolled in it weren't doing any better than the kids who didn't. A special assistant to the president, Norman Johnson, thought he knew why. He explained, "We were starting off with the idea that the kids were dumb. We didn't say that, of course, but the program was set up on a deficit model. We were going to fix what was wrong with these minority kids." Johnson suggested changing the concept from a pre-enrollment "remedial" course to a college-prep course, along the lines of pre-season athletic training.

Within five years, the results of this shift were remarkable. In the 1992 freshman class twenty-one minority students—fourteen blacks and seven Hispanics—finished the year with a perfect 4.0 average. In this one year, more minority students achieved a 4.0 than in the entire decade from 1980 to 1990. Moreover, 10 percent of the minority student population—as opposed to 5 percent of the white students—had achieved a perfect average. As a result of this impact, white students have demanded the opportunity to enroll in the program and colleges throughout the nation came to recognize Challenge as a blueprint for their own "bridge" programs.

On the level of elementary students' performance, the same relationship between expectation and academic acceleration holds true. In New Jersey—a state where student performance in public schools is notoriously dismal—children at an independent inner-city school, the Chad School, have excelled in the sciences and math, although 75 percent of them come from single-parent households with incomes below the poverty line. Chad School's emphasis on excellence continues even into its "summer camp," where the curriculum is not limited to conventional recreational activities but also stresses science and high-tech training, which its young students eagerly devour.

In spite of this remarkable history of self-help and current examples of excellence, many spokesmen for the black community who are heavily invested in a culture of victimhood find it strategically undesirable to recognize or herald success. In the past, successful blacks maintained a close relationship with black colleges, whose publications featured periodic updates on black entrepreneurial victories. These success stories gradually disappeared as a victim mentality took hold and permeated the black community.

Sociologist John Sibley Butler describes the turn of black academics to a culture of victimhood as follows:

> After slavery, most of the research on black Americans was in a category called "racial uplift." This research was designed to show the progress of black Americans in the area of education, institutional building, the creation of societies, and business enterprise. Although there was research done on problems associated with black America, it is clear that the racial uplift literature balanced, and indeed outweighed the literature on the problems. . . . Around the late 1970s, research on black Americans made a complete shift to the study of failure within a hostile racial society. Like a city covered after an earthquake, most of the success of black America was buried and forgotten.[8]

It is true that since the post-Civil War era, it has been necessary to document racial disparities and discrimination in order to make a case for civil rights protection. However, since the 1960s, this focus on grievances has taken on a life of its own, dominated the debate, and eclipsed the documentation of black successes. Black spokesmen have turned away from the rich legacy of a past that was spiritually and economically vibrant and looked, instead, to legislation and politicians for salvation.

In fact, evidence of an alternative route to black progress—one that stresses individual initiative, mutual cooperation, and self-help—has not only been ignored but has suffered outright attacks from black leadership circles that have big stakes in the message of victimhood.

One colleague, the Reverend Buster Soaries, whose oratory and example have fanned the flames of a moral brushfire among black youths, calls this the "Lazarus Syndrome." He explains that, if Lazarus had just stayed dead, the Pharisees would have eulogized him, built a park in his honor, named a street after him, and maybe even declared a National Lazarus Day. But when he was raised from the dead, Lazarus became a threat to the powers of his day. He was evidence of the Truth, and those who found the Truth uncomfortable saw only one course of action: they plotted to kill him.

Since the mid-1800s, a tension has existed between two factions within the black community—those who believe that racial equality should be pursued through the avenues of integration and legislative initiatives and those who believe in the power of self-determination and believe that stable and lasting racial equity must be based on a foundation of economic achievement. At the turn of the century, these two camps were epitomized in the figures of W. E. B. Du Bois—who focused on civil rights, the right to vote, and the intellectual development of the "most talented" blacks—and

Booker T. Washington—who stressed the primacy of achieving economic stability. The heat of the friction between these two men and their philosophies was clearly evident in Washington's 1895 presentation at the Atlanta Exposition. In his address at this event, Washington applauded the "opportunity afforded to awaken among us a new era of industrial progress" and dismissed Du Bois' talented-tenth strategy:

> *Ignorant and inexperienced, it is not strange that in the first years of our new life we began at the top instead of at the bottom; that a seat in Congress or the state legislature was more sought than real estate or industrial skill; that the political convention or stump speaking had more attractions than starting a dairy farm or truck garden. . . . Our greatest danger is that in the great leap from slavery to freedom we may overlook the fact that the masses of us are to live by the productions of our hands, and fail to keep in mind that we shall prosper in proportion as we learn to draw the line between the superficial and the substantial.*

Washington went so far in this speech as to offer to trade black Americans' quest for equal rights and integration in return for a promise by whites to allow black Americans to share the economic growth of the South.[9] It was this step that allowed his opposition to label the speech the "Atlanta Compromise" and to dismiss Washington as an "Uncle Tom."

When I traveled to Ghana several years ago, I searched out the grave site of W. E. B. Du Bois—who had turned to socialism in his later life and died in exile. Standing among the weeds that had grown up near the simple stone marker, I was struck by the difference in the legacies that these two men had left: one a lonely grave site in a distant African land; the other, the endowed Tuskeegee University.

Perhaps no other figure who pursued black self-determination and rejected an agenda of integration met with more vehemence from the NAACP than Marcus Garvey. Garvey's belief that collaborative effort could ensure black progress led him to launch the Universal Negro Improvement Association (UNIA), the Negro Factories Corporation, and a newspaper, *The Negro World,* which promoted his goals of racial solidarity and resettlement in Africa. As a model of what could be accomplished through self-reliance, Garvey went on to launch the first black-owned steamship corporation, the Black Star Line, which was financed by one-dollar investments from more than three million black shareholders. Garvey's rejection of integration strategies had been a thorn in the side of the NAACP, but the remarkable mass appeal of this steamship project made him appear even more ominous to other black leaders. For some time, they countered his efforts with ad hominem attacks, such as Du Bois's description of Garvey as "A little, fat black man, ugly, but with intelligent eyes and a big head." However, when more than 25,000 enthusiastic blacks gathered at Madison Square Garden in 1920 for Garvey's "First International Convention of Negro Peoples of the World," the NAACP launched an attack designed to silence Garvey's competition for leadership. In January 1923, eight leaders of a campaign entitled "Garvey Must Go" wrote a letter to the U.S. attorney general, urging him to break up the UNIA and to convict Garvey, whom they charged with false advertising of his Black Star Line.

Although the judge who tried Garvey, Julian Mack, was a member of the NAACP—a key player in the effort to oust the activist—Mack insisted on trying the case. The trial lasted one month. Garvey was convicted and eventually exiled.

The entrepreneurial genius S. B. Fuller was yet another model of personal responsibility and self-help who met the wrath of the civil rights establishment. Although for many Americans the words "Fuller Brush" connotes a white door-to-door salesman ringing the doorbells of a suburban neighborhood, this dynamic company was launched in 1935 by an enterprising, visionary young black man who had only a sixth-grade education and twenty-five dollars in his pocket. S. B. Fuller knew the power of perseverance and personal effort. Not only did his Fuller Products Company survive and thrive during an era of debilitating racial discrimination, but his enterprises eventually grew to include eight other corporations—among them, the Courier Newspaper Chain (with papers in Pittsburgh, New York, Detroit, and Chicago), a Chicago department store, and a New York real estate trust.

Fuller's life experience was vivid evidence that victimhood was not the only road open to black Americans, and in a public address to the National Association of Manufacturers in 1963, he issued a scathing indictment of those who hold that racism is the sole culprit to blame for the problems of the black community. His speech read, in part, as follows:

> . . . *It is contrary to the laws of nature for man to stand still: He must move forward or the eternal march of progress will force him backward. This the Negro has failed to understand. He believes that the lack of civil rights legislation and the lack of integration have kept him back. But this is not true. . . . In 1952, the Negro's income was 57% of that of the white man's, but in*

1962 it was only 53% of his income. In a period of ten years, the Negro's income had dropped four percentage points in comparison with the white man's income. The main reason for this is the Negro's lack of understanding of our capitalist system of government. . . . Unfortunately, the Negro believes that there is a racial barrier in America which keeps him from succeeding, yet if he would learn to use the laws of observation, concentration, memory, reason, and action, he would realize that there is a world of opportunity right in his own community. Since the Negro does not supply the demand in his own community, the white man must come in, and he takes advantage of the opportunity. Then the Negro thinks that there is a racial barrier that keeps him from making progress. Therefore, he asks for legislation to remove the barrier which he automatically created himself, due to the lack of action in his own behalf.[10]

In a later interview, Fuller criticized civil rights leaders for misleading blacks, charging that their leadership was "shallow and irrelevant," and caricatured them as "standing before the white man with a handful of gimmees and a mouthful of much obliged." Incensed, the civil rights leadership called for a boycott of Fuller's businesses. Shortly thereafter, Fuller was the target of an investigation in which he was charged with violating several provisions of the Federal Securities Act.

I, too, have had direct confrontations with the civil rights establishment who have disdainfully labeled strategies of self-help and personal responsibility "conservative." In 1994, when I spoke before a conference of black journalists in Atlanta and refused to join the civil rights establishment in attacking Supreme Court Justice Clarence Thomas for his critique of affirmative action, Ben Chavis lashed out, accusing me of being an "intellectual prostitute." This incident resulted in an editorial by Cynthia Tucker of the *Atlanta Constitution*, which read in part:

> *You might think the executive director of the National Association for the Advancement of Colored People would embrace the concept of diversity. After all, as a prominent black activist, the Rev. Benjamin F. Chavis Jr. would be expected to advance the idea that a broad range of opinions and perspectives ought to be included in any discussion of social policy.*
>
> *But Chavis, like many African-American politicians and activists, is not so interested in diversity, it seems. On the contrary, he exhibits an active disdain for diverse political views among black intellectuals. . . . Chavis did not stop at merely disagreeing with Woodson or Thomas, which would have been legitimate, perhaps even appropriate. Instead, Chavis launched a personal attack on Woodson. . . . [11]*

Civil rights leaders who focus myopically on the transgressions of white America have ignored the heritage of once close-knit, strongly moral black communities and thriving black business districts. They have replaced this model with another portrait of black America. The message that young people now receive from many of their purported leaders is that, because racism exists, they should not be asked to merit their rewards or to take responsibility for their wrongdoings. "You are a victim of society," they are told. "If you rape your sister, or rob or kill your brother, it's not your fault."

In too many cases, blacks in leadership positions have pulled out their civil rights credit cards when they have been charged with personal indiscretions. When former Congressman Gus Savage was charged with sexually harassing a young black Peace Corps worker while he was on a diplomatic visit in Africa, he defended himself as being "targeted" by racists. No voice among the members of the Black Congressional Caucus rose to reprimand him and, in fact, a number of Caucus members campaigned for his reelection. Similarly, when former Congressman Mel Reynolds was charged with having sex with a sixteen-year-old campaign worker, Reynolds's defense was that he was the victim of the racial bias of a politically motivated white prosecutor.

Throughout history, black America's most powerful leaders never used racism as an excuse for their failures and would not use the moral authority of the quest for equal opportunity as a shield in personal affairs. Even when the Reverend Martin Luther King was blatantly harassed and when his phone conversations were illegally taped by J. Edgar Hoover, King never enlisted his massive nationwide network of supporters to come to his defense in personal matters. Yet today, when it is so important to stress the importance of self-determination and personal responsibility, many black leaders point the finger of blame at racists and environmental factors to excuse their own criminal action. And the upcoming generation is invited to do the same. Tragically, many young blacks act on this message.

Recently a legal defense of "urban distress syndrome" has been developed to excuse young blacks who have murdered other youths. According to the advocates of the syndrome defense, youths who murder are simply automatons functioning in an environment where the rule is kill or be killed. Gone are the notions of free will, moral standards, and the possibility rising above sociological determinism.

As a culture of victimhood has replaced a once-solid conviction in personal responsibility, the moral foundation of a once-invincible black community has been compromised.

When I appeared on Black Entertainment Television with Jesse Jackson, I referred to the strides that blacks had made in spite of historical racial oppression much worse than today's. When I stressed that these achievements were due to hard work, not affirmative action or "generous white people," Jackson disagreed. So I challenged him: "Are you suggesting that the destiny and history of black America has been determined by what white America has allowed us to do?" His reply? "Abso-DAMN-lutely!"

Accepting an identity as "victims" has done more damage than years of outright discrimination could accomplish, because it has caused destruction from within. We have fallen prey to an epidemic of an entitlement mentality. A victimizer may have knocked us down, but it is up to us to stand up again.

The single most devastating effect of all of the culture of victimhood is the abandonment of the morality, ethics, and personal responsibility which was the glue that once held the black community together.

At a time when the nation as a whole is undergoing a spiritual crisis, and when an upcoming generation—rich and poor, black and white—is drifting without moral moorings, black youths have been the most vulnerable population. They, above all, have been indoctrinated with the message of impotency and irresponsibility and have been taught that their failures or misdeeds are due to factors and enemies on the outside. They have been denied a legacy of self-determination and personal responsibility that could be key to their survival.

Today, many "leaders" of the black community continue to preach that racism is the main cause of the problems that plague our people. This claim has been devastating because a fixation on racism has prevented a probe of the root cause of the crisis we now face. The plagues that are dooming our future—black-on-black fratricide, a generation of children who will never receive love from the fathers they will never know, lives wasted through drug and alcohol addictions—these are all ultimately spiritual problems. The blame for these tragedies cannot be laid at the feet of white America.

Today, there is a vacuum of spiritual leadership and a dearth of models of personal responsibility. Even many leaders of the black church—once the anchor of mutual aid, industriousness, and moral stability—seem to have checked their spirituality at the door for the sake of political alliances and mutually beneficial relationships with the poverty industry.

Some pastors have become the most adamant defenders of the poverty industry, in spite of the devastation it has wreaked on their people. For example, a consortium of black ministers have been among the most vehement opponents of a welfare reform initiative in Michigan which would have empowered neighborhood-based organizations—including faith-based groups—as service providers in their communities. These ministers were the antithesis of their predecessors in the church who once provided a hub for progress and philanthropy in their communities. In a public letter to Governor John Engler they declared: "The role of the churches is and should be to do all in their power to see to it that the State fulfills its responsibility for all its citizens. . . . Furthermore, government employees equipped with social service skills are the appropriate people to administer our health and social welfare programs and funds—not volunteers from among our congregations. It is outside our responsibility and beyond our capability to do what you are suggesting."

In this vacuum of responsibility, where can we now go for moral leadership to address the spiritual decline and moral free-fall the society is now experiencing? We must seek out the Josephs of our day.

Chapter 4

Modern-Day Josephs

Who They Are
and
What They Do

Like their biblical counterpart, many modern-day Josephs have emerged from the bondage of oppressive circumstances. One by one, they have been called to lives of responsibility and service—from jails, from drug addictions, from lives of crime, prostitution, and violence. For some, this was the kind of lightning-strike conversion that Juan Rivera described: "I hit the canvas, and when I stood up I was, forever, a different man." For others, change took place by increments, step-by-step towards productive, liberated lives.

Whatever the differences in the transformation process of our modern-day Josephs, they all hold a number of important characteristics in common. First and foremost, they all refused to let external circumstances control their destinies: regardless of the odds they faced, they refused to accept the label of victim. Most underwent a personal, internal transformation, after which they dedicated themselves to helping others in similar circumstances achieve productive, fruitful lives.

The stories of our modern-day Josephs provide a paradigm and model for addressing the spiritual crisis that afflicts our society today. These Josephs have forged an effective internal, spiritual response to the spiritual and moral atrophy of our civil society which goes far beyond the limitations of conventional remedies of professional therapy and economic assistance. Many effective grassroots approaches of personal and community revitalization are faith-based. Even those that are not rooted in a particular religion have a spiritual component in the tireless, heartfelt commitment of grassroots leaders and their unwavering confidence in the potential of every human being.

The work of today's Josephs may not be buttressed with bound volumes of data and file drawers of client profiles, but, more importantly, it is supported by the undeniable transformations that have taken place in the lives of the people they have served. Grassroots Josephs may not have degrees and certifications on their walls, but they do have this—the powerful, uncontestable testimonies of people whose lives have been salvaged through their work. The undeniable fact that lives have been transformed through the work of modern-day Josephs must be appreciated even by observers who may be skeptical about their approach.

We should embrace and pursue this evidence with the same hope and vigor with which we pursue breakthroughs in the arenas of medicine or technology. Our advanced Western doctors have been willing to research any promise of a cure for an epidemic such as AIDS. If, out of a laboratory of thousands of mice, just three did not develop the disease when exposed to it, we would never dismiss those mice as "inexplicable aberrations." We would invest all the time, energy, and expertise we had to determine what variables were different in the case of those immune mice and how we could reproduce that immunity.

Medical researchers have traveled as far as Tibet to seek cures for medical conditions that afflict our society. In fact, a number of the tranquilizers and sedatives that our doctors currently prescribe evolved from studies of Tibetan monks who used certain herbs to calm frenzied dancers after tribal rituals.

One recent milestone in the ongoing battle against cancer, a chemotherapy compound called CPT-11, which was recently approved by the Food and Drug Administration, was developed by a Japanese yogurt company that specializes in desserts, cosmetics, and a yogurt-like health drink. In spite of its unlikely source, the drug proved to be effective in treating some of the sickest cancer patients. In tests, from 40 to 60 percent of patients whose colorectal cancer had spread to distant sites such as their livers or lungs had their tumors stabilized. Now hailed by some specialists as "the most important anticancer drug to come along in quite some time," the compound was developed over a period of four decades. In 1957, 1,000 plant samples were shipped to the National Cancer Institute, which was seeking plants and trees that might contain anti-cancer agents. A year later, a handful of the 1,000 samples—those from a Chinese tree—were found to have tumor-suppressing power. Forty years of research was invested in the study of a tree grown in a distant country, although there was only a tiny thread of hope that this research would yield a cure. Far less than 1 percent of the trees studied had curative characteristics, but even this thin thread of hope sparked intense interest and years of diligent study. Although the breakthrough was finally made by a company that was far removed from the arena of Western medicine, the result was welcomed without regard to the credentials of the people who discovered it.

It is a tragedy that this same openness to unexpected sources of solutions, which has generated much of our progress in the fields of science and medicine, does not expand to the arena of societal dysfunction. Professional sociologists and psychotherapists dismiss many grassroots successes in transforming wasted lives as simply the effects of isolated examples of charismatic leaders and go no further to probe the possibility of expanding and exporting their success.

I will never forget the experience I had when I attended a conference of one grassroots, faith-based substance abuse program in Texas. One by one, more than fifty men and women approached the microphone and stated only two simple, but powerful, facts: the number of years they had been addicted to heroin or crack, and the number of years they had been freed from their addictions through participation in that program. Many of these former addicts have gone on to become the directors of satellite centers of that program and have themselves salvaged hundreds of lives. This is not what I'd call an isolated charismatic aberration. Yet, because this specific program is based on Christian principles, it has been downplayed or ignored within the realm of professional therapy. In a society where God is sometimes more feared than guns, there is a reluctance to accept the validity of a faith-based approach, regardless of the impact that it may have on thousands of lives.

Some critics of scriptural-based drug treatment argue that such solutions can only work for those who are already predisposed to a faith-based strategy. Yet the testimonies of hundreds of men and women who have experienced dra-

matic turnarounds in their lives reveal that many of the people who were ultimately freed of their addictions through
faith-based programs had previously been hostile to religion
and spirituality.

In contrast to many secular substance abuse programs that
try to establish reputations for success by accepting only
clients who have a good chance of recovery, most grassroots
programs have worked with the people that all other
groups—the churches, clinics, and psychologists and psychiatrists—had considered hopeless. Their doors are open to
those who are deemed "too far gone," or "beyond the age of
rehabilitation." Today's "Josephs" have embraced them all—
prostitutes, thugs, those whom society has labeled value-
less—and they have changed their lives. They have proven
that they could reach people who were in the absolute abyss.
Among those I have met who have prospered through a second chance at life are a drug-addicted thief whose own
mother slept with her purse under her mattress, fearing that
he would rob her, and a heroin addict who "shot up" his own
son when he was just fourteen—a son who by the time he was
eighteen was serving time with him at the same penitentiary.
These lives were salvaged. These people were "called to
themselves" and began lives of service.

Still, there is a reluctance to embrace faith-based approaches because they are seen as "irrational." This criticism
fails to take into account the fact that the problems they are
addressing are also fundamentally irrational. It is not rational
for a celebrated athlete with a multi-million-dollar contract or
for actors and actresses at the peak of their success to decide
to inhale cocaine, knowing that it will probably, in time, de-
stroy their lives and careers. The addiction to drugs and alcohol that has devastated the lives of thousands of individuals

and their families is the result of irrationality. Its remedy, likewise, may lie beyond the calculations of cool reason.

It is remarkable that we can understand and accept it when men and women give up their lives to death by taking drugs. We are used to witnessing men and women whose lives are given over to darkness through addictions in which they become totally different people, leaving their families, becoming strangers to their loved ones, abandoning their jobs and careers, losing their reputations, and, finally, succumbing to prison or death. We accept this type of transformation as a phenomenon of life. But we refuse to acknowledge the validity of a rebirth to life and light. We close down when someone says, "I have been born again. I may have done things that have been self-destructive and devastating for others, but through the transforming power of Christ, I am a new person. My relationship with my mother, my father, my sister, my spouse, my sons and daughters has changed." Society will not accept that type of rebirth.

"Just Say No" campaigns and advertisements in which frying eggs represent a drug-coddled brain fail to educate or frighten people into a responsible lifestyle. Why do they fail? Because they rest on the false assumption that the problem is a lack of the information needed to make correct life choices. But when a doctor or a pharmacist decides to take drugs, his or her problem cannot be solved by education. Those individuals had all the information they needed to make a rational choice, but their decisions were irrational.

We have only to look at the comparative success rates of grassroots intervention and conventional therapeutic programs to appreciate what today's Josephs have to offer. Many faith-based substance-abuse initiatives, for example, have success rates as high as 70 and 80 percent, while the success rates of most secular therapeutic programs hover in the single digits. A comparison of recidivism rates of the two types of approach would reveal even greater evidence of the long-term impact of faith-based programs. This is due not only to a difference in the approach that is used but also to a fundamental difference in the goals of each.

The goal of most conventional programs for substance abuse and violence intervention is termed "rehabilitation." In reality, the type of rehabilitation produced by these programs amounts to no more than simply restoring a client to the state he was in before he exhibited social deviance. But there is no reason to expect that an individual in that state who was previously susceptible to the temptations of drugs or alcohol would not be susceptible again when he is returned to his original condition. Statistics show that when these rehabilitated individuals reenter their dysfunctional environments they are likely to return to old patterns of behavior.

Not long ago, for example, a youth who had been declared by a judge to be "not innocent" in the murder of a cab driver in Washington, D.C., was sent for therapy in a psychiatric treatment center near Lake Placid, New York. After receiving professional therapy at a cost of more than $100,000 a year, that young man walked away from the low-security facility and returned to Washington where he murdered a convenience-store clerk, just blocks away from his first homicide. This youth's therapist claimed that he had made some progress, because he exhibited some signs of regret regarding the second murder.

In contrast with psychological therapy and treatment that relies on medication, the goal of grassroots programs is not rehabilitation but "transformation." These programs, the majority of which are faith-based, do not seek simply to modify behavior but to engender a change in the values and hearts of the people they work with which will, in turn, affect behavior. Unlike the volatile effects of behavior modification, the impact of a transformation lasts a lifetime. The neighborhood-based programs that inspire transformation do not simply curb deviant behavior but offer something more—a fulfilling life that eclipses the power of temptation. When transformed individuals reenter their old environments, most do not become recidivists, and many have had the power to change those environments.

An analogy can be made between a dysfunctional life style and a plot of land that has been overtaken by weeds. Rehabilitating that land would be simply clearing away the weeds, leaving the soil in the state it was in before they began to grow. In essence, this is doing no more than tilling the soil. The newly turned ground will be even more susceptible to weeds than it was in the first place. As the Bible warns, if an evil is banished from a house but nothing is given to take its place, that house will be filled with an evil seven times greater.

By contrast, in the process of transformation, grassroots leaders do not only eliminate the weeds but plant good seeds in their place. There will be no place for weeds to take root if a plot of land is filled with lush grass. Juan Rivera is a man who personally has experienced transformation. I once asked him what safeguards he takes to prevent himself from drifting back into his drug addiction. He answered,

> I've had my share of heartbreaks and temptations. I had a younger brother who was shot and killed about three years after I came to Christianity and it was a childhood friend of mine who killed him. About four years ago, I had a sister killed. Those were times in my life when I asked, "How can this be happening to me?" And then thoughts would come to my mind—that powerful temptation, you know, "What you need to do is you need to go out and get a fix: You need to go out

and smoke some rock. You need to go out and do this or do that to alleviate this pain." But I tell myself, "You've got too much to lose . . . in this life that's been given to you—in this life that you've found." What helps me is that I know what I have and I know what I'd be going back to. I've been there. I know what would happen to me the moment that I decide to go back to drugs—the moment that I decide to go back to the streets. That's a safeguard for me. And I'll say no and I'll always just turn around and just keep moving forward.

Juan Rivera had lost seven years of his life to heroin addiction. His days were spent in burglaries to support his habit. His nights were lost in a haze of drugs. But in 1972, the seeds were sown for a transformation in his life.

Today, he recalls a fateful morning when he was sitting, barebacked and shoeless, on a curb in front of the single-room shack he was living in. As a result of his addiction, his features were skeletal, his eyes hollow, and his hair was long and matted. Juan lit his first cigarette and began thinking about what house he would burglarize that day. "I preferred to do my burglaries in the morning," he recounts, "The earlier the better. I'd just stake out a house until the parents and children left. I felt the night was made for other things. Suddenly, I found myself thinking on a deeper level, thinking about what I'd do with my life if I had another chance and about all the things I would have wanted to accomplish." But then he stopped and caught himself, and remembered, "Once an addict, always an addict." He had tried and failed to escape his addiction before. He had changed his location, undergone therapy and taken medication. He was convinced now that nothing would work.

Juan was turned off by religion and wasn't about to pray about his life. But this longing for change sent out a message that was answered. Several months later, when he was at a court hearing, he met a man named Freddie Garcia, who told him that he was operating a program for addicts called Victory Home on the southwest side of San Antonio, Texas. Freddie explained that he had once been an addict himself, and as he named some of the drug sources he had used, Juan recognized their street names and began to trust Freddie and to open up—until Freddie said that his addiction ended when he accepted Jesus Christ. Juan closed down. But he pocketed the card that Freddie had given him.

Months later, Juan was caught by the San Antonio police in a drug sweep. This was not the first time and, as Juan explains, most addicts treat a periodic lock-up as an occupational hazard. "Every drug addict knows that the best thing to do after a raid like that is just to lay back and take advantage of the wonderful generosity of taxpayers and look for a federally funded program. . . . Addicts enter treatment, get on Methadone and, in return, entertain the psychiatrists and sociologists. The trick is to just play along with the system until all the pushers are out of jail and reinstated on the streets. Then the addicts leave the treatment programs and the whole cycle starts over again."

Juan found Freddie's card and decided to use the program for his temporary stop-off. He put in a call and within fifteen minutes Freddie had arrived to pick him up. Soon after that, Juan found himself in a worship service with Freddie at the podium. He recalls,

> *Everyone was singing songs, clapping, shouting, doing all kinds of crazy things. Then Freddie began to preach and asked us to bow our heads and said "Jesus is here this morning. If you're tired of living the life you're living, Jesus is here and he wants to exchange your old life for a new one."*

Juan panicked. His main thought was that his friends would never accept him if he "got religious." He recalls "I was the lowest—a criminal and a drug addict—but I was afraid that if I became a Christian I'd get a bad reputation." Still, he knew he was tired of his life . . . something had to change. He found himself asking for forgiveness. Juan explains, "I didn't have a spiritual experience. I didn't see bright lights or have an out-of-body experience or anything, but something inside me changed that day. I didn't progressively stop using drugs, stop burglarizing, or stop drinking. Those desires just left me that morning."

Freed of those desires, Juan knew he had to be in a place where his resolve and will power could be nurtured and strengthened. He continued to live at the Victory Home with others who were recovering. In each of Victory Fellowship's facilities, key support is offered by "house parents," a married couple who live with the men and women who are striving to end their addictions. Unlike professional counselors who come in at 8:00 A.M. and leave at 4:00 P.M. and disappear on holidays and weekends, these parent figures are personally committed to the people they serve and are available twenty-four hours a day, seven days a week, providing the direction, discipline, authority, and love necessary for those who are born again to grow again.

For Juan, who came to Victory Fellowship at an early stage in its development, that parent role was fulfilled by Freddie Garcia and his wife Ninfa. In Juan's words:

"When I read the book of Joseph, first of all, I see Freddie. Out of the many things we can learn from Joseph, he was a patriarch in the true meaning of the word. He was a provider. He was a man who made provision for others. I see that in Freddie. Even in his servitude, he was the best steward. He made provisions."

Today Juan has committed his life to passing on to others what Freddie had given to him. He explains:

I always tell those guys, if you learn to live first, then you can learn how to make a living and not fail. We have all seen professionals who have failed miserably in their families, homes, and marriages. I tell them that home-base needs to be taken care of first. In the book of Acts, in preparing people to receive the spirit, Paul says, the purpose of this is so that you can be witnesses. So you can go out first in Jerusalem, Judea, and Samaria and then in the outermost parts of the world. Why did he say Jerusalem first? Because that was home base. Take care of home first. Get this nailed down. Then you can go out into the community, then you can move out into the city, and then out into the country.

I ask these guys, How many times have you done things backward? You go out and get a job, you go to school, or you're working, but you eventually come back to your old ways. You will always come back if you look for external solutions first. The problem is not in the economy, or housing, or racism. Those are only byproducts and symptoms of a greater problem that exists, and that problem is in you. Now, once that problem is taken care of in you, then you can be successful in anything. I feel—not from arrogance but honesty—that today I could venture off into any profession I want and I believe that I would be successful. Because I have learned how to live. And that is what sustains me. That is the sustaining power in my life that Freddie taught me through classroom instruction and through example: How to live. I learned how to live.

Juan recalls that in his days as an addict, he had actually passed by the Garcias' Victory Home. When he saw groups of men in the yard he had thought it was a drug outlet! From his experience it was too humble a place to be a rehab facility. Juan says, "I had been in an out of rehab facilities and I knew what they looked like. When I looked at Freddie's I didn't see any reception building, no administrative offices, no security station." In truth, Victory Fellowship performs its miracles on a shoestring budget in very modest facilities. The program draws addicts seeking to be freed from all across the country, and it has never turned anyone away. It is often so crowded that program participants sleep in tents. Hardcore addicts who are suffering the ordeal of going "cold turkey" are given cots in a trailer. Dinners of rice and beans for more than a hundred people simmer in two big pots on the stove. But though the physical conditions of Victory Fellowship are spartan, it is rich in the compassion and love that make transformation possible.

Juan explains that a fundamental element of bringing an addict back to life is engendering a sensitivity to others by having him take responsibility for another person. In Juan's words,

> *When these guys were addicts, they saw everything and everyone—even their wives and children—only in terms of how they could feed their addictions. Part of their recovery involves a commitment to others who are trying to end their addictions. They keep a vigil of prayer and caregiving over the cots of newcomers who are breaking hard-core addictions. In that process, something happens. A part of their heart opens and they have, for the first time in years, a sensitivity to the condition of another person. I have seen men who had been hardened by life, men who have stolen and even killed, come to me sobbing if the person they were trying to save didn't make it and went back to the streets.*

Victory Fellowship founder Freddie Garcia's depth of heart as a counselor and guide was forged in the crucible of his own addiction. A passage from his autobiography captures the hopelessness that plagued his life before he underwent the transformation he has since inspired in thousands of other individuals:

> I took our baby Josie along with me on burglaries and when I went to score. One hot humid morning, after scoring, I drove to the nearest gas station, took Josie into the men's rest room and put her down on the wet cement floor while I prepared my fix. I was tense and in pain. The sweat ran into my eyes and burned, blurring my vision. Nothing went right. Josie started to cry. Someone banged at the door, wanting to use the rest room. I pierced my arm over and over, missing the vein. I felt like screaming at my four-month-old baby—but then the needle hit a vein.
>
> At once, every muscle in my body relaxed. I felt good, but glancing in the mirror, I saw myself—hollow cheeked and unshaven. I hadn't bathed for several days and the odor of my own body nauseated me. I bent down to pick up my little girl from her "bed" of dirty toilet paper. The foul stench tore at my nostrils, but she was smiling at me, her big eyes brimming with tears, her hands reaching up. "Man, how did I get this low?" I whispered as I held her close. "I never wanted it this way, my little baby."[1]

Freddie could never have known then that his future would hold a life-giving transformation, which would spread like a moral brushfire among all those who would come to him.

Juan Rivera stayed with Victory Fellowship until his own healing was complete—and then for another twenty-three years in service to other addicts and alcoholics. He eventually married Freddie and Ninfa's daughter, Josie, and has become Freddie Garcia's righthand-man in an international ministry.

Victory Fellowship had a big mission but very humble beginnings. The Garcias began their outreach thirty years ago in their own tiny one-bedroom house where buckets and bowls caught the drips during rainfalls. At one point, all the living room furniture was moved under a makeshift awning outside the house to make room for eleven recovering addicts who slept on the living room floor. Now, after thirty years of service, the program has freed more than 13,000 men and women from their addictions and has spread to sixty-five satellite centers in California, Texas, New Mexico, Peru, Puerto Rico, Mexico, Colombia, and Venezuela.

The faith-based transformation of Victory Fellowship begins at a point of spiritual conversion with an acceptance of personal responsibility and a desire for forgiveness, but this does not mean that the program is nebulous or left up to the flow of the spirit. Victory Fellowship has expanded with clear goals and a practical, strategic plan to realize them. A visitor at Victory Fellowship's headquarters would be impressed with the catalogued tapes of inspirational speeches and sermons that occupy a wall of bookshelves and with the order and care that are evident in even the smallest details of the facility.

The overarching goal of every program affiliated with Victory Fellowship is restoration and support for the family. Where this can only be a long-term goal, programs create a family-like environment to offer personal support, care, and example. Today, Victory Fellowship's outreach includes numerous drop-in centers that function as safe havens for youths in eight public housing developments, a gang-intervention program, a program for youths in the juvenile justice system, a network of drug rehabilitation homes with a head-quarters in San Antonio, a campus outreach, and jail and prison ministries. The Royal Rangers and Missionettes, Victory Fellowship's versions of the Boy Scouts and Girl Scouts, offer character-building, community-service projects for children aged five through seventeen. Freddie Garcia is also the pastor of the Victory Temple Church with a congregation of eight hundred members, 60 percent of whom were formerly drug- or alcohol-dependent.

Not long ago, my family spent our Easter vacation in San Antonio with the Garcias at Victory Fellowship. One day, after we'd finished a picnic lunch, Ninfa gave her car keys to three graduates of the program who had overcome drug addiction and asked if they'd take my twelve-year-old daughter and her two young grandchildren to an amusement park and a movie. They drove off assuring us they'd be back by 9:00 P.M. I was certain, as Ninfa and Freddie were, that our kids were in good hands. I asked myself how many psychiatrists or therapists or social workers would have such confidence in their treatment that they would entrust their own children to their clients?

Although Freddie's leadership provided the core of this massive outreach, as it continues to expand, Freddie is always in the process of raising up other leaders and training them to choose and develop their own cadres of leaders. In one training session, Freddie's sermon on "Choosing Men for Leadership Positions" contained the following guidelines: Choose men who have a heart of love. Everything else can be taught—how to speak publicly, management techniques, and even, if necessary, how to read. Choose men whom people are already following. That is evidence that they have a heart of service and that people trust them and are attracted to them. Choose people of warm and friendly attitudes, not those who look like they'd been "baptized in lemon juice."

Freddie's "lemon juice" metaphor is just one example of his humor and sense of perspective—qualities that he shares with hundreds of other grassroots leaders. Some of my most enjoyable evenings have been spent in pre-conference, late-night rap sessions with grassroots leaders, whose laughter and humor can best be appreciated by fellow public servants who have made the same sacrifices, taken the same risks, experienced the same victories, and suffered the same defeats. At one such session, Freddie told of some newly recovered converts and some snafus they encountered when they began their lives of service.

Because community service and ministry are part of the recovery process, Freddie told us, residents of the Victory Home sometimes go to hospitals to pray for the sick. On one occasion, two recovering addicts were praying fervently over a terminally ill elderly woman in a hospital. As they finished their prayer, they realized that the woman had passed away. Fearful that they were somehow responsible, they escaped through the nearest window.

In another instance, a group of musicians from Victory Home had been invited to perform at a funeral. When they returned in the evening, Freddie had questioned them, saying that the family had called, concerned because they had not come as scheduled. Further investigation revealed that they had mistakenly performed at the wrong funeral! The funeral director thought that the family had asked the group to play, until the family expressed gratitude to the funeral director for having made arrangements for the musicians to come.

This humor, some differences of opinion, and occasional mistakes, attest to the human element of the conversion process. Freddie and his large extended "family" do not claim to be perfect and they don't think in terms of celebrity or position—they want only the freedom and opportunity to serve.

In addition to many overtly faith-based programs such as the Garcias' there are also many grassroots leaders whose outreach is motivated by a heartfelt spirit of service but is not affiliated with any particular religion or faith. And, although many of the most effective grassroots healing agents have personally experienced the lives of depredation and corruption that they urge others to escape, there are also among our modern-day "Josephs" those who have never even ridden on a stolen bicycle. There are as many different types of Josephs as there are different kinds of needs. However, despite the broad variety of the sources of inspiration and the life experiences that motivate today's Josephs, they all hold a number of defining characteristics in common.

1. Their programs are open to all comers. The grassroots leaders do not target their services exclusively to individuals of any particular race or background. Help is offered, instead, on the basis of the need a person has and his or her desire to change.
2. Neighborhood healers have the same "zip code" as the people they serve. They have a firsthand knowledge of the problems they live with, and they have a personal stake in the success of their solutions.
3. Their approach is flexible. They know that every person cannot be reached in exactly the same way. Even where there may be a pervasive theology or philosophy in a program, not every person is expected to embrace it or be affected by it in the same way.
4. Effective grassroots programs contain an essential element

of reciprocity. They do not practice blind charity but require something in return from the individuals they serve.

5. Clear behavioral guidelines and discipline play an important part in their programs. I will never forget the sight of former felons and addicts washing pots and pans at Victory Fellowship or scrubbing down pews in restitution for some violation of the program's rules. Previously, neither the threat of a death sentence nor life imprisonment meant anything to these individuals who accepted homicides as a fact of life and who anticipated a life span under thirty years. Yet they had willingly accepted the discipline of an unpretentious, Hispanic sixty-year-old "Joseph" because he had won their trust.

6. Grassroots healers fulfill the role of a parent, providing not only authority and structure, but also the love that is necessary for an individual to undergo healing, growth, and development. Like a parent, their love is unconditional and resilient. They never withdraw their support, in spite of backsliding and even in the face of betrayal.

7. Grassroots leaders are committed for the long haul. Most of them began their outreach with their own meager resources. They are committed for a lifetime, not for the duration of a grant that funds a program.

8. Today's Josephs are available. In contrast to a therapist who comes once a week for a forty-five-minute session, or staff who are there only from nine to five and then return to their distant homes, grassroots leaders are on call virtually twenty-four hours a day. Their homes are open to the people they serve, who are seen as friends, not as clients.

9. The healing they offer involves an immersion in an environment of care and mutual support with a community of individuals who are trying to accomplish the same changes in their lives.

10. These Josephs are united in a brotherhood of service. They are eager to share ideas and strategies. They offer earnest support to each other in times of struggle and sincerely celebrate one another's victories.

Thousands of miles from San Antonio where Freddie Garcia was performing his daily miracles, another Joseph responded to a call to service in Hartford, Connecticut. Like Freddie, Carl Hardrick has worked to meet the needs of his low-income neighborhood for more than thirty years. He shares the same heart of service that the Garcias embody, although his outreach is not based on any particular religion or theology.

In 1967, Carl had become active in the South Arsenal Neighborhood Development Corporation (SAND) in Hartford at a time when the bulldozers of urban renewal were devastating the community and leaving many public housing families looking for a place to live. Of 640 public housing units that had been scheduled for construction, funds were allotted to build only 240. Various neighborhood groups joined together under the banner of SAND, which became a powerful lobbying group that won not only improvement in housing conditions but also better city services and more street lights to improve neighborhood security. As SAND achieved recognition and respect for its role in tackling community problems, it eventually moved to address the growing problem of youth crime and gang activity in the inner city.

Carl was strongly drawn to this area of SAND's activity, for gang violence was taking a greater toll than all of the other environmental conditions combined. Through links with people in the neighborhood, Carl learned the structure of the different gangs and became familiar with their chains of command. Like most other grassroots leaders who have been effective in quelling gang warfare, he understood that it was important to work through the fulcrum points of the leadership.

As friction between the various gangs began to mount in the summer of 1975, shots were fired into a crowded fast food restaurant. The attack was aimed at members of Hartford's largest, most notorious gang, the Magnificent Twenties, but barely missed two innocent customers who were standing in line. Carl knew that the violence would escalate uncontrollably unless he took quick action, so he immediately sent out word through the street network that he wanted to meet with the Twenties' leader, Steve Holter, at a room in a community center. Carl himself was amazed at the response and the extent of the teenaged Holter's power. As he recalls,

The Twenties had always bragged of a membership of nine hundred but I'd always thought they were bluffing. That night, when Steve Holter walked into the room, he was followed by a literal stream of his gang members. They kept coming and coming. I thought they'd never stop. In school, Steve had been labeled as a slow learner and a problem student, but his ability to control and organize a following like that was evidence of his genius and his potential.

As a result of that night's meeting, the Twenties agreed to send representatives to rendezvous with members of the rival gang. The next night, Carl, Steve, and four Twenties got out of their van in the designated parking lot. But rather than being met by a similar cohort from the other gang, they found themselves surrounded by more than two hundred of their armed rivals. Carl didn't flinch, and demanded a second meeting, in accordance with the agreement that had been arranged. The circle broke up and the gang members dispersed and met again later on neutral turf to discuss a truce. As Holter explains, "When we were able to talk about our differences, we found out that a lot of our fights resulted from rumors that had no basis in reality. We began to realize the seriousness of the situation, and, finally, we reached a truce."

Impressed by Carl Hardrick's commitment and resolve, Steve gradually began to trust, respect, and listen to him. As this leader of the most powerful gang began to change course, a strong contingent of the gang followed his lead. It had not been an attraction to violence and warfare, but a need for a sense of belonging and identity that had drawn these youths to gangs in the first place. This feeling of unity and identity was preserved, even as the direction of the gang's activity changed dramatically. Steve recalls, "We were tired of the ugliness. We turned from night to day like a light switch."

Once the bane of their community, the Twenties began to invest their energy and talent in community service. Understandably, the residents did not immediately trust this transformation. Carl explains, "When the neighborhood residents launched a Community Youth Day, the Twenties asked to participate. But the neighbors knew the kids' reputation and decided against it. In spite of being excluded, the gang chipped in for a donation of $250 that they presented to the event's organizers. Gradually public perception began to change. The Twenties delivered turkeys to the elderly and needy at Thanksgiving and hosted a Halloween party for the younger kids. Steve recalls, "As we began to change our course of action, it had a ripple effect on the young brothers who, even in elementary school, were imitating us. We began trying to raise some money by establishing a couple of discos. Carl convinced us that we could make more money by inviting people from around the area to come, so we invited other gangs. We set a rule that everyone had to check their weapons at the door. So there they were in the coat room— guns, knives, and sticks with tags on them. We enforced our own rules. There was no liquor, no smoking, no swearing. If someone came in drunk, he could get a refund, but he had to leave."

Members of the gang also brought their street knowledge and influence to the public arena, serving on various boards and political organizations. Steve Holter took advantage of job training opportunities through the local public housing authority and eventually became a partner in a construction business, Relph & Holter Homebuilders, Inc., which has survived and thrived and now provides construction training and jobs for other youths in the community. Steve also has become active in outreach to direct young people to productive lives, speaking in schools, meeting youths in prisons and detention facilities, and talking to the kids he meets on the streets. His success has made him a role model and his message echoes the guidance Carl once gave him. "You can make a difference in this chaotic world. It won't be easy. You may need help yourself, but no one can walk over that bridge for you. Life is about choices."

Although Steve describes his turnaround as a night-and-day change, like every transformation, his required years of nurturing and support from Carl throughout periods of challenges and backsliding, before it firmly took root. Through all of the tribulations of development, Carl never gave up on Steve. But Carl's greatest challenge did not involve his trust in Steve's potential, but a threat to his own commitment to nonviolence. One night, word came to Carl that his own brother had been jumped and beaten and that he was in intensive care, paralyzed. Steve went to the hospital with Carl and stood with him at the foot of the bed as his brother cried, pleading with him to take revenge. Carl's resolve was destroyed. As they went down the elevator, he was set to get his gun, when Steve spoke with the same sincerity and honesty that Carl had always invested in him, "Carl, you know if you decide to take those guys out, I will stand with you. But if you do, everything you have told us all for years will mean nothing." Carl knew he could not retaliate.

Now, years later, Carl Hardrick is still reaching and changing the lives of a new generation of young people in the city of Hartford. In March 1996, Carl traveled to Washington, D.C., with five redirected gang members who came to testify at a conference of policymakers and to spread the word of peace among high school students. The five, Herman "Big Bird" Cintron, Kendall "Bookman" Hardy, Chan Williams-Bey, David Carrasquillo, and Geanie Kase, who stood side by side and encouraged one another throughout their presentations, had been leaders of two of Hartford's most notorious rival gangs, Los Solidos, and 20 Love. Geanie, once the leader of a female branch of Los Solidos, told an audience of teenagers about her plans to open a laundromat. She had taken a job in a local laundromat to gain experience and "learn the lay of the land." "In our neighborhoods," she explained, "people don't have houses with laundry rooms and washers and dryers. There's a great need for safe, clean laundromats." She also told of impressive plans to launch franchises and even sell stocks in her business in the future. "I just knew I'd be doin' time in federal prison if I didn't change, and God gave me a second chance."

Carl Hardrick does not take credit for the dramatic turnabouts that have been inspired through his efforts. Instead, he talks about the influence that the youths have had on each other and of their mutual support: "I knew if I could reach Big Bird, he could reach Geanie, and that if they become successful, it will affect the 'Hood." Still, it would greatly lighten Carl's load if his tireless efforts with Hartford's youths could elicit some recompense. Like many other neighborhood healers, Carl has not been able to secure an occupation that is in line with his vocation. While his nights and free time are devoted to transforming and redirecting young lives, his days are spent completing health inspections of restaurants in order to support his wife and children.

Antonette "Toni" McIlwain is yet another modern-day "Joseph" who has been a catalyst for a remarkable revitalization of her Detroit neighborhood of Ravendale. Under her leadership, residents in thirty-five of the thirty-eight blocks in her neighborhood have organized with block captains and special committees. As a result of their efforts, crime in the area has been reduced by 42 percent, drug traffickers have been driven out, and a community park now stands where a notorious crack house once operated. The well-lit, landscaped neighborhood bears little resemblance to the devastated, disinvested area it was before Toni planted the seeds of commitment and hope among her neighbors. And Toni, herself, is far different from the person she once was—an abused wife and distraught mother of four small children.

Years ago, Toni had been so worn down by years of beatings and verbal abuse from her husband that she could see no hope of escape. Her self-confidence had been shattered, and she had been blocked from establishing any relationships that might have given her counsel and support. Toni had been tempted with thoughts of suicide, but when her husband shot at her and the bullet grazed her face, fear for the safety of her children moved her into action, and she determined that she would either get out, or die trying to escape. She gathered her children together and slipped out of the house. In the panic of the moment, she left even her children's shoes behind. Toni recalls:

We had no place to stay and nothing to eat. We ended up staying in an abandoned house that had been pretty much destroyed in a fire.

Sometimes I would plead with a shopkeeper for some noodles, and he'd give us whatever he could spare. One day, the store was closed so I went around to the back dumpster, hoping to find something for my kids. As I opened the lid, a rat jumped out with a chicken in its mouth. I was both angry and humiliated because that rat had got to the food before I had, and I knelt down and cried and prayed, "Just give me a chance and I'll prove that I'm worthy. Just show me some light at the end of the tunnel."

I knew a couple of people who lived downtown and I'd sometimes beg for bus fare and go down to see if there was any way they could help us out. I was waiting for the bus one day, looking raggedy and skinny and wearing a pair of slippers when I met Roger. At that time, Roger was fighting his own battles with drug addiction, but he had a house just down the street from where we were sleeping and when he found out I had four kids, he gave me a key to the place so that I could give the kids baths and feed them there.

I wanted so much to put my life together. I wanted to go back to school, but the people at social services told me that my kids were too young for me to think about that. . . . So I found a course myself, just by looking through the yellow pages. I found a work incentive program where I could get a high school degree and further my education. I had also seen a help wanted sign at a dry cleaners, and took a day job, from 10 to

6, working with my kids playing in back of the counter. My classes started at 6:30. When I finally got my GED I felt like a thousand-pound weight had been lifted from my chest. I went on to business school and earned a degree—two degrees! I was on a roll!

Toni continued to use Roger's home as a respite for her children but, she remembers,

It took me a long time to begin to trust him because of everything I had gone through. Then one day Roger came home and overheard me singing to the kids. I wanted to give them a sense of hope and security and so that's the way I always put them to sleep . . . by singing songs—positive songs. But because of what he had grown up in, Roger had never experienced that before, and he was moved. That was the beginning of a breakthrough in opening up to each other.

Within several months, Toni and Roger were married. They were able to purchase a home through a program in which they made a nominal down payment and then applied their rent payments to the purchase price.

Toni was proud to finally be a homeowner, but when she tried get to know her neighbors, she realized that residents were skeptical of her outreach. When she approached one woman working in her yard and introduced herself, the woman shut her off saying, "Didn't anyone ask you your name." The neighbors had decided that the best way to get by was to live and let live.

But the neighborhood was deteriorating and it was getting more and more dangerous. Absentee landlords were letting their properties slide into irrevocable disrepair and many were abandoning them. Drug addicts were stripping vacant houses of everything from plumbing and wiring to doors and windows. Crack houses were multiplying. One former dealer identified thirty crack houses in the thirty-eight-block neighborhood, describing one as a drug addict's version of a fast food restaurant: "You could get any thing you wanted in any amount. You could use it there or do a carry-out." Out of hopelessness and fear for their own safety, the neighbors had decided to just look the other way.

Toni, who had firsthand experience of individual transformation, also believed that community transformation was possible if there was determination and hope. She walked door to door, urging residents to turn out for a community organizational meeting to be held in her living room. She called out to neighbors who looked down from windows with iron security bars and she called out her message through the locked front doors of more timid neighbors.

On the night of the first "meeting," Toni and Roger sat alone in their living room. Three subsequent meetings failed to bring the neighbors out. However, on the afternoon of the fifth meeting, a friend loaned Toni a bullhorn and she bravely strode up and down the streets, calling out, "Whatever you're doing in there—Put down that forkful of eggs! Put down that newspaper you're reading! Come to the meeting on Wade Street and we can change this neighborhood."

Whether it was the authority of the bull horn or the cumulative effect of Toni's persistent efforts, the "walls of Jericho" began to weaken during this march around the neighborhood, and residents arrived at Toni's door. Toni had a simple immediate goal—to improve the security on her block by improving the lighting. She had made arrangements with a wholesaler to purchase lawn lamps at a discount price and asked only that neighbors contribute a $25 down payment for their cost. She had also asked an electrician to volunteer his services to install the lamps. One by one, the street lamps appeared on Toni's street, until the entire block was well lit.

One youth who had formerly been a dealer in the neighborhood pointed to the rows of gleaming lights and said, "This street is different. See that light? It says 'I care.' And that one? And that one? 'I care. I care. I care.' This is one block where no dealer would want to come. No one would come and stand under one of those lights."

Inspired by a new sense of hope and community, the neighbors brought out rakes and shovels and brooms and paint brushes. In small brigades, they hauled litter and debris from alleys and cut back plants and grasses. With newly painted curbs, litter-free streets, and landscaped lawns, Wade Street stood in striking contrast to the rest of the neighborhood. One neighbor, an artist, contributed two signs which were hung at either end of the block, announcing, "Welcome to the 'United Neighbors of Wade.'"

Toni explained, "We used a different yardstick to measure a person's value. You may collect trash, but if you are a good trash collector you are part of what makes this neighborhood special. One former athlete has set up a recreational and sports program for young people; one neighbor makes our signs; and one man set up a little candy shop for neighborhood children in his shed and contributes $25 a week to our community organization."

The Wade Street Block became a symbol of hope and empowerment for the neighborhood, and soon other neighbors became interested in the idea of block organizations.

One of the biggest challenges to the neighborhood was posed by the hundred abandoned or condemned houses—eighty-nine of which were HUD properties. These properties, which functioned as crack houses and were often gutted of anything of value (including plumbing, wiring, and bricks), were a primary cause of community blight. On some blocks, as many as four crack houses were in operation at the same time, some pulling in profits of more than $4,000 a day.

Toni and her neighbors had attempted to at least board up the houses to prevent vandals and dealers from entering, but federal regulations prohibited their efforts. The neighborhood association then decided to declare dominion by virtue of ownership. They pooled their resources and purchased a number of properties for the price of their back taxes. Then teams of the neighbors set to work, painting, fixing windows, and restoring the homes to livable conditions. With each house that was rehabilitated, one more center of drug trafficking was shut down and one more affordable home became available for low-income working families.

Drug trafficking was done also through occupied homes, where the dealers gave the tenant a portion of their profits in return for the use of the premises. The neighbors' first strategy was to notify the landlords of drug activity. In some cases, these warnings were ignored and resented by landlords who claimed that the neighbors' activity was an infringement on their privacy. In such cases, the neighborhood association took their battle to the next stage and called for police raids which sometimes resulted in the takeover of a property, sending out a message to other absentee landlords. A number of responsible landlords have been grateful for the neighbors' involvement and have even asked the "Ravenites" to screen prospective tenants.

Today, all but three blocks of Ravendale have been organized with block captains and committees. Monthly leadership training classes are ongoing throughout Ravendale for block club captains.

The police department has also been invited to participate

in the reclamation of the neighborhood. Through a "Cops on Patrolling the Streets" (COPS) program the police now provide security training, and a police mini-station has been established in Ravendale. In addition, an Automobile Theft Prevention Program has been created. The effects of these efforts are visible. Crime in the neighborhood has been reduced by 42 percent. As a testimony to the successful reclamation of their neighborhood, each year more than four hundred residents march in a national Night Out, hosted by the Detroit police department.

Rehab efforts also continue, often through an adopt-a-block program which links residents with congregants of a suburban church. In these joint efforts of inner-city renewal, Toni advises her neighbors to see themselves as givers as well as recipients. "Remember," she tells them, "you are learning from them but they are also learning from you." Toni has also developed a working relationship between the residents and local businesses and has written up a "contract" of mutual support in which both agree to work to improve the security and contribute to the economic and social uplift of the neighborhood. Grateful for the involvement of the citizenry, merchants contributed one hundred turkeys to the neighborhood association last Thanksgiving. A food bank established in conjunction with a local ministry, Joy of Jesus, has served more than five thousand families.

Rehab includes occupied as well as vacant houses. Through a Paint-Blitz program, teams of residents have moved through the neighborhood, giving a new look to more than 139 homes. In addition, a summer youth services program has been established, serving fifty young people each week who are offered courses in topics ranging from conflict resolution to community involvement.

Today, a caller to McIlwain's residence might be greeted

by a cheery voice on an answering machine from a buoyant, confident "Toni" who is light-years away from the woman who once searched dumpsters for scraps for her children. There is no more telling tribute to the victories this woman has claimed than the nature park, with landscaping and brick walkways provided by neighbors, which now stands on the site of a demolished crack house.

Eric Reavis, an eighteen-year-old who is now an active gang counselor, is another individual who has firsthand knowledge of the transforming power of today's "Josephs." Eric received his high school diploma several months ago and has also completed a number of preliminary college courses. He has already been accepted at the University of the District of Columbia in Washington, D.C., but has his sights set on Howard University. Sitting in an office at Washington's Dupont Circle, talking about effective gang prevention, Eric wears a blue dress shirt and his name tag from his day job at a medical facility. While going to school he also took a weekend job, selling ice cream near the Capitol mall. Eric's creativity and ingenuity are expressed even in this role as a part-time ice cream vendor. He tells of how he designed and printed small comment cards for customers, inscribed with his name and address. He says that the response to the cards surprised him.

> *Within a few weeks I received at least fifty notes from tourists who returned to their homes throughout the country, some with photos they took of me while they were in Washington. All the letters begin with "Dear Ice Cream Man!"*

Had it not been for guidance from modern-day Josephs, Eric would not be applying to college, would not be holding down two jobs, and most likely would not be alive. It is only recently that Eric's life has been filled with vision, productivity, and the freedom to pursue his dreams. Six years ago, his life had been set on a course in a tragically different direction.

Eric was born in Louisiana and raised with his two brothers by his maternal grandmother. When they were just eleven, twelve, and thirteen, the boys began to press the limits of authority and committed a number of petty thefts in their neighborhood. When they were apprehended, they were brought before a judge in juvenile court who was famous for his maxim of "zero tolerance" for crime.

The judge ordered Eric to leave his parish, and he was sent to live with an aunt in Texas. Once away from home, Eric gravitated towards youths who were rougher and bolder than the friends he had in Louisiana. Eric became a habitual juvenile offender who seemed overpowered by his own anger and resentment. He was sent to a psychiatric facility for observation and treatment.

Eric looks back at the time spent in that institution as excruciating. For the first time, he had lost his freedom and there was no certain prospect of release. He felt dehumanized—an object to be analyzed and documented—and had even been hooked up to electrodes by experts who studied the effect of his anger on his brain activity. Patients were put together in spite of a broad variety of behavioral problems. Eric recalls,

There was this one girl who would just go off in her violence. One day, she asked me once if I had any batteries and, thinking that she needed them for a radio, I gave her a couple. Then, right in front of me, she swallowed them. They rushed her for an emergency operation and had to cut her open to get the bat-

teries out. But just about a week later, before her incision was healed, she purposely ripped it open again.

I knew that I had to get out of that place, and another guy and I planned our escape. The only windows without bars were from a second story kitchen, so we decided to go out that way. We took sheets that we tied together so we could lower ourselves down, but the sheets ripped and I hit the ground hard. I bit my tongue in my fall and it was really bleeding, but we heard an alarm and we just ran and ran. We knew we had to get out of there. We came to a car and this kid I was with hot-wired it in less than a minute. That astounded me. I was a country boy from Louisiana and had never seen that done before.

Our first stop was at a liquor store. We figured that the alarm system was just a deterrent and that it wasn't connected to any other site so we broke in and grabbed some things from the shelves. I took mostly candy bars and things. The other kid was older, so he went for some of the beer. After we were on the road, I asked if he'd stop at a gas station so I could use the rest room. I came out after just a minute and didn't see the car. Suddenly someone grabbed me from behind. The police caught us that quickly.

Eric was out of therapy but in a juvenile facility, where he soon learned the rules of a separate, dangerous world. He remembers,

I was just standing in line waiting to be checked in, when I could hear a couple of the older guys talking about me saying "Look at that pretty face. We'll get that one." I knew I had to control myself and not say anything back. So I just stood expressionless and moved on. Later I found out about one guy who had come through and smiled at a group of those guys.

Within two weeks, he was gang raped. His whole life was messed up.

Life within the facility required a delicate balance. Eric learned when to calm himself and when to stand up for himself and preserve his dignity—even if a scuffle meant days or weeks in solitary confinement, or a year added to his sentence. Once, while waiting in a cafeteria line, Eric received an intimidating shove from the youth behind him. He knew that he had to retaliate to save face and to announce himself as off-limits for future assaults. A fist-fight ensued that resulted in an all-out riot. Eric found himself in the lonely emptiness of weeks of solitary confinement. He remembers that he counted every brick in the wall, over and over again.

Of those days, he says, "It got so I was just angry at everything and everyone . . . and I didn't trust anyone. I hated physical contact, even a handshake."

At that time, he was introduced to Amon Rashidi, an ex-offender who had turned his own life around and had been hired as a youth counselor. Eric describes his first encounter with Amon:

At first I didn't trust him. I had seen other people who had postured as our "advocates." But Amon could relate and identify with us. Amon knew us, he had done everything we had done, criminalwise, and he had pulled himself out of the gutter. He was real. The way he spoke. How he was. He didn't change in different situations with different people. Amon was the same way all the time. He had a close relationship with the warden and told him that whenever anything went down—like a riot—to put the OGs [old gangsters] in solitary confinement. That was tough love.

Eric continues,

> *Even when I rejected what he was doing, Amon didn't stop because he recognized what I couldn't see—my leadership abilities. I was totally blind to what I could be. But Amon came in with all kinds of information and all kinds of opportunity, always relating it back to the community. Even if I rejected what he was doing, he just wouldn't stop. He kept coming back. Once when I attacked a staff member and was put in solitary . . . they told me that someone was there to see me. It was Amon. I could see in his eyes that he was disappointed in what I'd done . . . and then I could feel the love that he kept giving.*

That was a turning point for Eric, and his first experience of trust. Gradually, he dared to open up to understand and accept what Amon had been offering—new vision and new enthusiasm for his life. Eric recalls, "Amon taught us to learn from everything and everybody. At group meetings he would put our chairs in circles and then have us move around so that our groups were interspersed. Crips were sitting by Bloods, blacks by Latinos and even members of the Aryan Nation. He read everything from Marcus Garvey to Adolf Hitler, and he taught us that we could learn from everything." As Eric began to respond to Amon's message, Amon gradually entrusted him with increasing responsibilities and asked him to serve on a special council that was created to deal with problems among his peers in the detention facility.

Amon's outreach was supported by two other men—Omar Jahwar and Gary Scott—who were also determined to help the incarcerated youths turn their lives around. Omar and Gary provided additional guidance and counsel to Eric during the critical period of his transformation. Through the support of these mentors, Eric was able not only to control his anger but also to free himself from racial animosities and resentments that had seethed within him for years. Eventually he became eligible for parole.

When Loretta Garrett, an aunt who lived in Washington, D.C., petitioned to have Eric placed with her, Eric took advantage of a policy that allowed parolees to be transferred out of state. As fortune had it, he ended up in the District, assigned to a parole officer, Tyrone Parker, who was himself an ex-offender and the co-founder of one of the city's most powerful youth intervention programs, the Alliance of Concerned Black Men. It may have been simply the luck of the draw that entrusted Eric to a parole officer who was determined to reclaim his future, or it may have been divine providence. In either case, Eric received the support and guidance he needed to continue to pursue his plans for the future. Today, with a steady job and exciting prospects for the future, Eric knows that he can still call on Tyrone at any time, twenty-four hours a day, for help, advice, and support.

As a teenager, Tyrone had personally experienced the devastation of youth violence. He was once seriously injured in street warfare and was admitted to a D.C. hospital in critical condition. Twenty years later, at the same time of the year, Tyrone's own son, Rodney, was shot and was admitted to the same hospital. Rodney did not live.

Today still suffering the pain of this loss, Tyrone recalls, "It was about 3 A.M. when my sister called to tell me that Rodney had been shot. It was so painful to know that he, like me, had been caught in that same senseless violence, and that, unlike me, he would never walk out of that hospital." Tyrone knew that hundreds of youths in the District were being killed each year and that there was no end in sight. He wanted to do something to stem the tide of that carnage, and just a year after Rodney's death he found a way.

Tyrone had been reunited with several friends he had grown up with in Washington. Like him, they had all, at some point in their lives, fallen into the abyss of drug addiction and criminal activity. Several had served time in prison. Yet each man, through his own unique course, had undergone an internal transformation and emerged with a new vision of what their lives and their community could be. As they talked about an even more callous and brutal youth violence that was now rising up, they decided to come together in an effort to salvage the lives of the young people in their community. This commitment was formalized as they launched the Alliance of Concerned Men, which since 1991 has helped more than two thousand young people to escape the lures of drugs, crime, and gang violence and to envision and pursue productive pathways for their lives. This unified, impassioned team possesses experience, empathy, and tireless commitment that have elicited trust and hope from young people whose hearts had been calloused and hardened (some would think irrevocably) through their life experiences.

In the winter of 1997, one youth homicide in the District had a powerful impact on each member of the Alliance. A twelve-year-old boy, Darryl Hall, had been abducted and beaten by neighborhood rivals as he walked home from school. His body was discovered several days later in a nearby ravine. He had been shot, execution style, in the back of his head. Like Tyrone, four members of the Alliance—James "Mac" Alsobrooks, Pete Jackson, Eric Johnson, and Arthur "Rico" Rush—could not be at peace unless they made some effort to prevent any retaliatory attack for Darryl's murder. Although they had not previously worked in the Benning Terrace public housing development where Darryl lived, they went forward with the same strategy that had been effective in other situations. For days they walked the streets, talking to the young people to identify those who had influence in each of the warring factions. Their earnest pleas to the youths gradually won their trust, and representatives of each side agreed to meet in neutral territory—the offices of my organization in northwest D.C. Suspicion and fear permeated the first closed-door meeting, which youths as young as twelve attended in bullet-proof vests. Over the next two weeks, however, the youths came together several more times, and gradually began to open up. On January 30, they publicly declared a peace pact. As a result, crime in the neighborhood decreased dramatically. Nearly two months later, there had not been one homicide in a community which previously had been notorious for its youth violence. A football field and playground that had been a deserted killing ground is now filled with the laughter of children. Residents declared that the neighborhood had not been alive like this since the sixties. The neighborhood mail carrier broke down in tears at the sight of kids who were formerly vicious enemies now joking and laughing together. The official who is currently functioning as a receiver for the District's Housing Department arranged to provide jobs for the young men refurbishing the neighborhood, removing graffiti, and landscaping. They eagerly seized the opportunity. Plans are underway to provide additional training for the youths and to link them with counterparts in other areas of the country, former gang leaders who are now functioning as mentors for other youths in their communities.

In addition to such personal outreach to young people in the District, the Alliance of Concerned Men recognizes the importance of the foundation of the family and have dedicated themselves to connecting young men and women with their fathers. The group established a program to link prison inmates to their families, urging them to fulfill their responsibilities as fathers and husbands even while incarcerated. They have witnessed dramatic and long-term turnarounds in both fathers and their children in the course of their work, as deep relationships have resulted from consistent visits and opportunities to open their hearts and share with each other.

Ever humble and eager to reach young people, Tyrone describes his dual roles as a parole counselor and founder of the Alliance for Concerned Men as a blessing in his life. As hundreds of youths are referred to him each year, he has been able to refer them to organizations where their talents can be tapped and utilized, and their lives transformed— through the consistent, heartfelt investment of a person who has walked in their shoes.

Today, Eric wants to return the gift of life and hope that was given to him. In the free time he has, he volunteers to help with the Alliance's efforts and has played an important role in the group's gang-intervention strategies. Fluent in the sign language of the gang culture and knowledgeable in the ways of street life, he has riveted the attention of large audiences of young people. He has even coordinated a powerful anti-gang theatrical presentation in which high school students are invited to survey a casket, then lift the lid only to find their own images reflected in a mirror—a grim reminder of the casualties claimed by the thoughtless violence of today's youth culture. Eric played a key role in the transformation of the Benning Terrace neighborhood described above. Having just recently accomplished his turnaround, he was a living example of the change that is possible. Just several years older than many of the youths the Alliance was working with, he was a bridge between the two generations—and between the two factions of youths. In one of their earliest meetings, when asked to join in a circle of prayer, two rivals refused to come together. Eric physically filled in the gap, putting his arms around each of the youths and closing the circle.

Eric's personal struggle and victory represent the dual prophesies for an entire generation of today's youths: one, a future of creativity, vision, and enthusiasm; the other, the doomed destiny of lives that are senselessly wasted. At the crossroads of those two destinies stand two figures—Joseph and the Pharaoh. One possesses the commitment, understanding, and heart that can guide individuals to lives of spiritual health, fulfillment, and service; the other possesses the resources, power, and influence that are necessary to support, export, and expand that mission of revitalization and salvation. If, today, pharaohs can emerge who have the humility and wisdom to embrace and support our modern-day Josephs, like ancient Egypt our land will prosper for four hundred years—and beyond.

Chapter 5

Joseph and Pharaoh

*An Alliance
to Save
the Nation*

The alliance between the Josephs of our nation's low-income communities and modern-day pharaohs requires nothing short of a fundamental paradigm shift—an essential change in the assumptions that have guided the relationships between individuals with resources and individuals in need of support. We can no longer look at this relationship as one between donors and recipients. We can no longer approach this relationship in terms of charity. Charity is not the model for the interchange between our nation's pharaohs and Josephs. In the Old Testament, the Pharaoh did not approach Joseph with charity. His goal was not to establish a welfare system for the people of Egypt or food stamps for Joseph's people. No, he said, "Let us come together to address this danger or it will consume us all."

Like their biblical counterpart, although today's Josephs deserve to be heeded by modern-day pharaohs—political leaders and leaders of the business community—their effectiveness is not dependent on such recognition. Long before support or acknowledgment came from the outside, the Josephs of our nation lived committed lives of service and accomplished miraculous changes in the lives of those they served. Yet an alliance between today's Josephs and pharaohs will allow their transforming efforts to expand and further develop, to the benefit of the entire society.

This type of partnership requires a major overhaul in how we view the poor. Policymakers on both the left and the right see the poor as hopelessly lost in a sea of pathology with few personal redeeming qualities. They assume that their only hope of rescue will come from the professionals and the intellectual elite and they cannot recognize the capacities that exist within America's low-income communities. As former Secretary of the U.S. Department of Education Bill Bennett once so aptly stated, "The left sees the poor only as victims, while the right sees them as aliens."

These assumptions about the poor have spawned a social economy that is predicated on custodianship. Food stamps determine what the poor are permitted to eat; public housing, where they will live; public schools, where their children will be educated; legal services, who their lawyers will be; and medicare, who their doctors will be. The poor are sentenced to live within an isolated subeconomy, an experiment in socialism within America, where they are treated as impotent children yet expected to function as responsible adults.

Fundamental reform will mean using the principles that drive our market economy also to guide our approach to societal challenges. In the market economy, competition is the force that drives progress. The introduction of competition is a welcomed catalyst for innovation and product refinement.

Consider the immense strides that have been made in computer technology, for example. In this age of rapid and ever-expanding technological advances it is hard to believe that the first all-electric computer (ENIAC), which was introduced just fifty years ago, occupied 15,000 square feet of floor space and contained 18,000 vacuum tubes. At that time, since few businesses had 15,000 square feet in their offices to spare and even fewer could afford the phenomenal cost of an ENIAC, two options existed: subsidize its use to allow more people to gain access to it, or support and encourage competition to refine the technology. Fortunately, we chose to do the latter and, as a result, hundreds of individuals and companies joined in the race to create smaller and more sophisticated computers. One consequence of all this experimentation was the development of today's lap-top computer, which is now in general use and has far greater capacity than its massive progenitor.

Were there winners and losers in this transition in technology? Most assuredly so. Among those who may have suffered immediate setbacks were the owners of the massive computers, their suppliers, the people who maintained them, and others in the industry that surrounded the old technology. But the decision of whether or not to progress could not be left up to them. Those with a vested interest in the old technology could not be relied on to dictate the pace of change. The winners, on the other hand, were the American people. Competition had improved quality and expanded access by lowering the costs of computers.

Comparable advancements could be made in the societal arena if we were willing to be guided by the same principles we respect in the marketplace, where rewards are won on the basis of outcomes. In a market economy the fundamental basis of all transaction is mutual benefit. Two or more entities engage in an exchange in which each party offers something of value to the other.

If this model of marketplace exchange were to be applied in the social arena, those who have position, resources, and influence—such as policymakers, scholars, and business leaders—would invite grassroots community leaders to the bargaining table, not as supplicants and applicants but as full partners in a mutually beneficial relationship.

PARTNERSHIPS WITH THE BUSINESS COMMUNITY

Now as never before, community leaders who have promoted healing and development in low-income areas have much of value to offer business owners and corporate executives. In the past, business was often depicted as the enemy of the "little people"—the low-income, entry-level workers. In the Industrial Age, there was a ready stream of workers capable of performing monotonous, repetitive tasks. At that time, unions rose up to protect the interests of these laborers, who could readily be fired.

Today, the landscape has changed dramatically, and the needs of business and the agendas of labor unions have shifted, producing a realignment of interests that is seldom recognized. Currently, nearly 90 percent of our economy is linked to human services, information, and communication. Businesses need a different type of worker, one who is capable of retraining every seven years and who is equipped in both skills and attitude to perform complex functions.

At the same time, the rise of the poverty industry has had a powerful impact. The interests of the unions of service providers often conflict with the efforts of low-income individuals to achieve self-sufficiency and economic progress. Where there has been such a conflict of interest, the unions have represented the interests of the professionals. It is ironic that organized labor, the historic champion of the

American working class, has now joined the ranks of the poverty profiteers.

In many low-income communities under the dominion of the poverty industry, a culture of dependency has undermined the values of responsibility and reliability that were once the backbone of the work force.

The vast majority of problems confronted by businesses today are related to human resources. Many employers cannot obtain the quality of people they need in order to operate successfully. Business owners in the hospitality industry and restaurateurs have told me that they could double their profits if they could get enough sober, solid, responsible employees. The issue isn't training. The problem is getting enough people for entry-level jobs who have work-ready attitudes and work-ready values. As the vice president of a telecommunications company wrote in a commentary in the *Wall Street Journal,*

> *It's not trained people that businesses need; it's dependable, hard workers. Just give me an unskilled but dependable person of character, and I'll take care of the rest. I can train a person to disassemble a phone: I can't train her not to get a bad attitude when she discovers that she's expected to come to work every day when the rest of us are here. I can train a worker to properly handle a PC board: I can't train him to show up sober or respect authority.*[1]

A base of loyal, honest, enthusiastic workers is what businesses desperately need because these qualities directly affect the quality of their services and products. Importantly, these qualities are all characteristics of the men and women who have undergone personal transformations through the guidance of a grassroots Joseph. A by-product of the effects that Josephs have on the lives of the people they serve is "marketable character." As the co-director of Victory Fellowship, Juan Rivera, once explained in a presentation to representatives of the National Restaurant Association:

> *You need reliable workers, and the people in my community need jobs. You can teach these guys what to "do" but if no one has taught them how to "be" there will be trouble. They're going to start stealing from you; they're going to start lying to you; they're going to start playing games with you, and you're going to have a lot of trouble with them because they don't know how to "be."*

The role that grassroots leaders can play as character references for reliable employees is evidenced in a fascinating pilot program that was launched recently in San Antonio. There, the owners of several major restaurants have made arrangements with Freddie Garcia's Victory Fellowship to hire the program's graduates. Both partners in this business arrangement have much to gain.

Victory Fellowship's graduates will be able to earn the incomes they need to take care of their families. They will also bring a number of benefits to their employers. First of all, they are a reliable and enthusiastic work force. They understand the importance of personal responsibility and self-discipline and they can be trusted to come to work consistently and to arrive promptly. The graduates of Victory Fellowship bring additional benefits to their employers. Many of them had previously established reputations on the street for being tough and knowledgeable about the criminal culture. This now can be beneficial to the restaurants that employ them. Potential predators may think twice about robbing a store or restaurant where people would know who they are. They would also be reluctant to assault a worker whose cousin, or brother, or close friend still wields power on the street. The agreement between restaurant owners and Victory Fellowship is just one example of the mutually beneficial partnerships that could be formed between businesses and grassroots community leaders.

A prospective employee who comes with a solid work ethic and an honest reliable character will have little trouble learning the practical skills necessary for the job. An incoming work force that has been simply shunted along through a public school system in an environment that ignores the development of spirit and character has little to offer prospective employers. Not long ago, for example, it was reported that the CitiCorp Bank had to screen fifteen hundred high school graduates to find just two hundred employees to do simple data entry. In another case, the New York Telephone Company had to screen two thousand applicants to get two hundred capable of doing basic entry-level work. This screening was expensive and time consuming. Businesses also have to spend billions of dollars in training expenses, and it has been estimated that they spend over $100 billion in drug prevention or rehabilitation programs for their employees each year. These companies could save much time and money if they entrusted the Josephs of their communities to identify prospective employees who were work-ready in both skills and attitude.

On a foundation of established trust, grassroots organizations, in turn, could also educate residents of their low-income communities about the value of the products and services offered by various companies, opening a viable, but untapped, market.

Security is another concern of companies that provide services in inner-city districts. The business expenses of Bell Atlantic, for example, escalated when a union contract required that they send a security guard with each repair crew going into inner-city areas. If graduates of neighborhood-based initiatives were hired to repair and wire phones in their communities, they would be their own security. The respect and the reputation that these individuals had established previously on the streets would remain with them as they enter the work force. It is unlikely that their trucks will be vandalized or they will be robbed while they are performing repair work in their own neighborhoods.

Many corporations are also suffering because a number of their antagonists have lobbied for excessive regulations on their business. For example, regulations now compel insurance companies to insure in high-risk locations. In these areas, banks and insurance companies have difficulty making the same kind of character judgments they make every day in middle- and upper-income areas. They don't know how to determine who should get a loan or who should be insured and, consequently, they have made their decisions based not on how people live but on where they live. Because they established policies on gross generalizations about the residents of low-income areas, they have been charged with red-lining.

With the help of grassroots leaders who have a personal knowledge of their neighborhoods, banks and insurance companies would be able to make reliable character judgments. The Josephs of these neighborhoods could guide them to identify islands of excellence and areas of competence within inner-city communities. They would then be able to engage those communities in the way they do others.

Banks want to make loans and insurance companies want

to insure properties. But if their decision makers are dealing with an unfamiliar culture and background, they may not know how to distinguish between a responsible entity and one that is not. The pressure on these companies is aggravated by the fact that many residents of low-income neighborhoods are black and Hispanic, and, therefore, those who are hostile to business have been able to portray the issue as an example of racial discrimination.

Bob Moore, a grassroots leader and director of the Washington-based Development Corporation of Columbia Heights, describes the important role that neighborhood-based organizations like his can play as a liaison between banks and lending institutions and the residents of inner-city communities:

> *Many banks have no idea what's going on in the community. They see a couple of guys on the corner and they get scared. They don't understand values in the neighborhood. They don't know what property sells for. They don't have a "feel for the deal" and it takes a long time to get anything done. They need to be hiring people from the community who have training but also a firsthand knowledge of the neighborhood.*
>
> *In the Columbia Heights community, forty non-profit groups have handled 80 percent of the affordable housing in the neighborhood. They have done $80 million dollars worth of projects and not one has gone "belly-up"—because they market their properties at the right price and they get the right people as buyers and renters, and train them in financial management and home maintenance before they move into a dwelling.*

Today's pharaohs need not embrace the faith or spiritual orientation of our nation's Josephs in order to appreciate and benefit from the real-world impact of their efforts. Today's pharaohs and Josephs can establish partnerships simply because it is good business.

Josephs are healing agents and neighborhood antibodies. If businesses, even motivated by their own interests, can join forces with them, providing financial support and technical assistance, there is a potential to create an entire immune system which will protect and preserve the health of our society. If we are to take this paradigm seriously and tap its full potential, there should be clusters of businesses coming together, sitting down with clusters of Joseph organizations, to determine what they could accomplish together.

A neighborhood organization like Victory Fellowship may need uniforms for its young people or educational equipment. Josephs need buses, buildings, technical assistance, and resources to continue and expand the services they provide. Although businesses currently donate millions of dollars to charity, often as little as 10 percent of private charitable dollars goes directly to a Joseph. Businesses that have foundations and corporate giving programs should invest in these grassroots service organizations, instead of paying ransom to the civil rights groups and other members of the iron triangle. They should cease making ransom payments to the liberal-leaning special interest groups that picket their offices or condemn them in the newspapers. Too many American businesses have entered a Faustian pact with virtual extortionists who say, in essence, "Pay us, and we promise not to picket or riot."

Grassroots leaders can be powerful friends of business in cases where the government attempts to overregulate it or unions attempt to control the work force. These actions are often taken in the name of the poor and the disadvantaged. The moral authority that has allowed antagonists of business to thrive is the assumption that they are acting in the interests of the poor. That's the moral capital that they draw on. But if businesses had a relationship with low-income leaders, that alliance could undermine the false moral authority exerted by antagonists of business. The iron triangle could no longer claim to be the legitimate representative of the poor. This has already happened in a number of cases where groups of low-income people have stood up and stated their own opinion about counterproductive policies that have been established in their name.

Businesses could also promote economic development in low-income areas. Through an alliance with grassroots leaders and organizations, they could become involved in efforts to stimulate entrepreneurship and reclaim once-active but now desolate inner-city business districts.

A model for this type of investment is the Columbia Heights District in Washington, D.C. This once thriving black business district had been devastated by urban renewal and by the riots that followed the assassination of Dr. Martin Luther King. Although narrowly focused federal housing programs failed miserably as an effort to stimulate community revitalization, a collaborative venture has now been initiated by businesses and neighborhood groups which has already brought the neighborhood to the beginning stages of a substantial turnaround. Several years ago, a comprehensive, coordinated strategy was launched to provide affordable housing, attract an income-mix of residents and homeowners, and generate retail development in the area. Those who have joined forces in this successful revitalization effort include the following: A local community development corporation, the Development Corporation of Columbia Heights, which provides firsthand knowledge of the problems to be solved and has a personal stake in the success of the project; private lenders and inter-mediaries such as the Local Initiatives Support Corporation (LISC), which provide front-end pre-development financing, subordinated low-interest debt, and capacity-building support; private developers who bring their experience and skills to the table; and the local government which utilizes federal housing and community development programs and city-owned land, reducing investment risk and attracting private investment.

One of the most impressive projects of the collaborative re-vitalization effort underway in the neighborhood is the Ne-hemiah Project, a $15 million undertaking shepherded by Bob Moore, the grassroots leader and executive director of the Development Corporation of Columbia Heights. This venture, which offers homeownership opportunities and re-tail services, is being launched by a consortium of nine non-profit developers, nine banks, LISC, several foundations, a national insurance company, Pepco, and a for-profit devel-oper. When the project's first fifteen new townhouses were made available for sale, 450 prospective buyers applied. The shopping center, still under construction, is now fully con-tracted with tenant businesses, several of which will be owned by neighborhood residents, including the first business owned and operated by neighborhood youth.

If we can ever stimulate a nationwide, continuing and ac-tive engagement of the pharaohs with our Josephs the possi-bilities of what we can accomplish are limitless.

PARTNERSHIPS AND PHILANTHROPY

The market principles that guide the collaborative ventures of the Josephs and pharaohs should also extend to the realm of private charity. Ideas of reciprocity, ultimate self-sufficiency and, above all, support for indigenous community organizations should provide a lodestar for a new type of charity.

Recently, from conservative corners, the idea of "effective compassion" has been posited as means of reforming counterproductive charity. It suggests replacing services provided by a distant, cumbersome, counterproductive bureaucracy with personalized, privatized services to the poor. Although this is a step in the right direction, it is still a flawed paradigm for strategies to aid the poor, for it still retains the image of the poor being "rescued" by agents from outside the community, rather than supporting the indigenous agents of health and healing that exist within low-income neighborhoods. This same pitfall is inherent in a recently announced initiative for "volunteerism" that has been promoted by many on both the left and the right.

For thirty years, an airlift from the "Poverty Pentagon" has parachuted programs into low-income neighborhoods. Residents of the communities impacted by these programs were assigned the role of passive recipients and they had no input in the design or implementation of remedies for their own problems. Not only were these programs often misdirected, they were also unnecessarily expensive due to the top-heavy bureaucracies of professionals who designed and delivered their services. Even worse, they actually weakened the natural support structures of low-income communities, because they bypassed and usurped the roles of the family, churches, and neighborhood associations. The indigenous supporting institutions of these neighborhoods had once promoted solid ethical principles and clear moral standards. This moral aspect of service was sanitized from the professional programs. Yet a solid foundation of values and clear moral principles is necessary for long-term, substantive revitalization of individuals and their neighborhoods.

The debilitating impact of the well-intentioned helping hand is graphically described by a colleague, John McKnight, who posits the following scenario in a quiet Midwestern prairie community:

Farmers and townspeople mourn the death of a mother, brother, son, or friend. The bereaved are joined by neighbors and kin. They meet grief together in lamentation, prayer and song. They call upon the words of the clergy and surround themselves with community. It is in these ways that they grieve and then go on with life. . . .

Into this prairie community the bereavement counselor ar- rives with the new grief technology. The counselor calls the in- vention a service and assures the prairie folk of its effectiveness and superiority by invoking the name of his great university while displaying a diploma and a license.

At first, we can imagine that the local people will be puzzled by the bereavement counselor's claims. However, the counselor will tell a few of them that the new technique is merely to assist the bereaved's community at the time of death. To some other prairie folk who are isolated or forgotten, the counselor will offer help in grief processing. These lonely souls will accept the intervention, mistaking the counselor for a friend.

For those who are penniless, the counselor will approach the County Board and advocate the "right to treatment" for these unfortunate souls. The right will be guaranteed by the Board's decision to reimburse those too poor to pay for coun- seling services.

There will be others, schooled to believe in the innovative new tools certified by universities and medical centers, who will seek out the bereavement counselor by force of habit. And one of these people will tell a bereaved neighbor who is unschooled

*that unless his grief is processed by a counselor, he will proba-
bly have major psychological problems in later life.*

*. . . Finally, one day the aged father of a local woman will
die. And the next-door neighbor will not drop by because he
doesn't want to interrupt the bereavement counselor. The
woman's kin will stay home because they will have learned that
only the bereavement counselor knows how to process grief in
the proper way. The local clergy will seek technical assistance
from the bereavement counselor to learn the correct form of service to deal with guilt and grief. And the grieving daughter
will know that it is only the bereavement counselor who really
cares for her, because only the bereavement counselor appears
when death visits this family. . . .[2]*

If the forces of "effective compassion" and volunteerism
do not move beyond the notion of "rescue" from the outside
and if they do not channel their support and seek guidance
from indigenous community institutions, they will simply be
replacing liberal paratroopers with conservative paratroopers. Regardless of the sincerity and personal quality of their
compassion, they will, likewise, injure with the helping hand.

The director of a shelter for battered women in a small
mountain town tells how she learned this lesson from an experience regarding a Christmas celebration at her home. As
Christmas approached, toys and clothing donated by local
businesses began to arrive at the shelter. Volunteers wrapped
and tagged the gifts for the children and placed them beneath the tree. On the day of the event, the director stood in
the back of the room and watched the presentation of the
Christmas gifts. She saw that the donors were beaming. The
volunteers and staff were smiling. Yet that same joy did not
seem to emanate from the mothers who stood by or even
from their children who were opening their gifts.

The director realized that the problem was not the gifts, which ranged from Barbie dolls to bicycles, but the fact that the mothers did not feel that they had contributed to the event and had no input regarding the gifts their children received.

The next year, the Christmas party was planned in a different way. Months before the holiday, the staff drew up lists of tasks, from cooking and cleaning to clerical work. Residents of the shelter who took on different tasks were paid with special vouchers. The gifts that were donated that year were displayed on shelves at the shelter's "gift store." Just before Christmas, the women took their vouchers and went shopping for presents for their children. The gifts the children received that year brought them more joy than ever before: Each present was an expression of a mother's love and investment.

The story about that shelter's Christmas celebration provides more than a model for gift giving at shelters. It provides a model that should be used to guide all efforts to support and uplift low-income individuals and communities. Outreach to the needy should always be offered in a way that recognizes and builds on the capacities of its recipients.

Even the currently popular trend toward mentoring can be debilitating to the longstanding support structures of low-income communities if it is not offered with a recognition of their value. Mentors and other outside volunteers ought to first seek out indigenous remedies—the Josephs, the healing agents—to find out what's already being done in that neighborhood. Assistance should support and energize the indigenous healing agents so that they become the primary agents of their own deliverance. Then if mentoring or charitable outreach is required, let it be in response to a request from the Josephs who live in those communities.

A true act of compassion does not require the surrender of self-respect in exchange for assistance. The principle of reciprocity should guide the philanthropic exchange just as it guides exchange in the market place. People who are constantly on the receiving end, who have never been given the opportunity to reciprocate, will in due time despise not only the gift, but also the gift giver. Grassroots leaders and healers always require and demand a return on their investment from the people they assist. Passive recipients make "good clients" but poor citizens.

The situation of the mothers in that rural women's shelter provides a metaphor for the situation of grassroots public servants in low-income communities throughout the nation. Many of these community leaders have selflessly served their neighborhoods for years, often using only their own scant resources. They have a heartfelt commitment to the people they serve and they long to provide more opportunities than their funds allow. Tragically, when help from the outside arrives, it often bypasses them completely, as mentors and programs implemented by strangers go around them to the young people they had worked with for years. Like the gifts chosen and wrapped by strangers, when this aid is given from people who are available only from nine to five, and when these programs are implemented by professionals who have not established a bond of trust, they have negligible impact.

Truly "effective compassion" is charity that is directed in the right way, as a support rather than an alternative to the longstanding heartfelt service offered by men and women who live in the community. When resources and support are given to individuals who have a personal and long-term commitment to the people they serve, each donation will create ripples of benefits for years—and generations—to come. Like capital wisely invested, it will stimulate the moral and spiritual economy of low-income communities.

In Dade County, Florida, for example, there lives a woman named Dorothy Perry, who is affectionately known as the Mother Teresa of public housing. For more than twenty years, she has sheltered hundreds of neighborhood children who come to her humble housing unit after school for tutoring, Bible study, counseling, and love. Many are refugees from abusive homes where parents are drug addicts. Others come from families where parents need help in raising their children.

As a project of community outreach, Dorothy and her children formed a choir called the Singing Angels whose performances carry an uplifting, anti-drug message. Several years ago, my organization, the National Center for Neighborhood Enterprise, invited Ms. Perry and her forty Singing Angels to come to Washington to perform. We did not ask Dorothy for a list of the children so we could make arrangements for them. Instead, we gave Dorothy the air tickets and let her appoint the chaperons. We empowered her. The children arrived smiling and cleaving to Dorothy. It was "Aunt Dot" who took them to Washington—with the help of the National Center.

We must understand the importance of supporting the natural immune system in our nation's communities—the healing agents who are already working in those neighborhoods. We should be helping the "Dorothy Perrys" to secure the facilities, transportation, and educational and recreational equipment that could expand their neighborhood programs. We should get accountants to help them and should bring to their efforts the organization and sound management practices that can ensure their longevity. We should take care to do this in a way that does not force them to become overly bureaucratic. We should tap the technical support that is available from the outside, not to mentor their children, but to build institutional supports around the grassroots leaders so that they can develop a staff to recruit mentors from their neighborhoods. If the neighborhood leaders choose to invite outside mentors, let them come into their homes to serve their communities.

Although it is important that support is given through established networks of service within low-income communities, the proper relationship between today's pharaohs and Josephs must go even beyond the concept of "effective compassion," or well-directed charitable outreach. The very notions of "compassion" and "charity" connote a one-way avenue from the gift giver to the receiver. In truth, the Josephs of today have something to give to society that is far more valuable than anything they receive. In an era of spiritual hunger and moral disarray, today's Josephs are a source of both spiritual and economic renewal that will have an impact beyond the boundaries of their neighborhoods. Grassroots leaders who have proven that they can engender substantial and lasting transformations at only a fraction of the cost of less effective but "credentialed" programs have much to bring to the table.

It is important to distinguish such grassroots faith-based outreach from other social programs that may have a religious affiliation, such as larger, institutionalized charities sponsored by churches or sectarian cult-like organizations. In many cases, large, professionalized programs, regardless of their religious affiliation, are highly bureaucratic and are virtually extensions of the poverty industry, from which they receive the bulk of their funding. Often, like the established poverty industry, their goal is custodianship and maintenance of the poor rather than enabling the poor to achieve self-sufficiency.

Likewise, a cult-like group can be identified in terms of its goal and effect. If the purpose of an organization is only indoctrination and the expansion of its membership, it will not have the liberating, enabling effect that the Josephs of our day have.

The hallmark of a Joseph organization is its effectiveness and positive outcome. Josephs have been able to tackle the most entrenched societal problems that everyone, regardless of religious belief, recognizes as problems. It is safe to say, for example, that no one would argue that an alcoholic should remain an alcoholic. There is society-wide agreement that alcoholism and drug addiction are problems because they devastate the lives of addicts and their families and they are a destructive force in the larger society. The success that Josephs have claimed against these afflictions must be recognized as a positive thing by all members of society.

If an organization can take a dependent, destructive, and self-destructive individual and transform that person into a responsible, productive, contributing member of society, that organization or program should be recognized, supported, and embraced. This effectiveness is a defining quality of a Joseph. It is an undeniable fact that the vast majority of today's Josephs, those with the greatest positive impact on the individuals they serve, are faith-based neighborhood leaders and their organizations.

The proper relationship between today's pharaohs and Josephs is a mutually beneficial partnership based on a confluence of interests. Nowhere is this more evident than in the prospects for relationships that could be established between the business community and grassroots organizations that are agents of revitalization, but philanthropic outreach and public policy should also be designed in a way to support this fundamental partnership between the Josephs and the pharaohs. Former HUD secretary Jack Kemp is one political leader who understands the importance of this role. The policies he has consistently pursued through the many years of his career have been based on a recognition of the capacities that exist within low-income areas, and the potential benefits that grass-roots leaders can bring to society. On a number of occasions he arrived at my office for meetings with residents of public housing, legal pad in hand, eager to take notes of their recommendations for public policy and their understanding of the problems that face our community.

The Josephs of our day do not need charity. They need to be considered as "friends." The relationship of friends in every arena of society, working to pursue common goals, is a relationship that will allow America to heal and prosper.

Why Pharaoh Will Be Moved to Act

Just as there are two types of Josephs—those whose mettle was forged in "the crucible," who suffered and overcame the same afflictions as the people they help, and those who refused the lures of societal deviation against the same odds—there are also two types of pharaohs. In addition to leaders of the business community who have a material, financial incentive to enter such a relationship, there are pharaohs who may not have wealth but have standing in the academic and political communities who can be powerful policy advocates. They are like ambassadors. These pharaohs have the ability to perceive the internal, spiritual resources that grassroots healers possess and these pharaohs can be the voice that educates middle- and upper-income white America about the important role that the Josephs can play, not only in their own neighborhoods but also in the personal lives of the occupants of the gilded ghettos of our society. Throughout the nation, there are many individuals who are wealthy and white and powerful, yet are faced with emptiness and disarray in their personal lives. Many have children who are experiencing the same moral confusion that poor kids are feeling. This is a deeper point of common concern and the most fundamental need for the services that Josephs can provide. Josephs' ambassadors can convey to concerned and troubled middle-income parents, to the leaders of corporations, to the residents of lavish homes that echo with emptiness the message that, within low-income communities, there are grassroots servants who hold remedies for the crises they are facing.

There will be many pharaohs who, in spite of their seeming success, will have the humility and personal strength to admit "I have some of the same failings and shortcomings that low-income people do. I am having the same problem with my own son or daughter: I'm worried about drugs; I'm worried about some of their activities; and I'm worried that he or she may be suicidal. I'm worried and I'm looking for remedies. If I can find remedies among the Josephs in low-income neighborhoods, I'm going to look there." We want to say to those people that the Pastor Garcias, the Carl Hardricks, the Toni McIlwains—the Josephs of this world—have a remedy for them as well.

The Josephs of Amerca have discovered the healing remedy that can salvage this nation. This can't be overemphasized. They have successfully addressed the problems that everyone else says are at the core of our meltdown—the moral degeneracy that gets expressed in violence, spouse abuse, child abuse, drug addiction, prostitution. They have been especially successful in attacking the problem of drug abuse, which is our most threatening problem and the incarnation of evil itself, because it destroys a person's fundamental value system and structure. It is only these "new" people, these transformed Josephs, who have the answers to the problems of drugs, alcohol, violence—all the problems that plague our society. As an entire society, we must organize ourselves in such a way that we can reach out and harness this vital resource and nurture it. We must come to a point where we can understand and seek out the power that would be unleashed if we were to nurture and embrace the Josephs of the world. We should understand that these societal antibodies can help not only low-income people, but also our own children. They can help us heal our own broken marriages and dissolving families. They can do for us what education and power and influence have been unable to do.

It is critical for us to recognize the power of our nation's Josephs. This is not just a book about how we can solve poverty. The Josephs of this world have found the cures for the apathy, despair, and isolation that are ripping apart all families, regardless of income and race or social position. If America's inner-city Josephs can heal the hurt that is in the heart of a hard-core drug addict who has been to prison and who once refused to yield to the authority of the police and the warden and society—if they can heal a person who has been so severely damaged and hardened, imagine what they can do for those who have gone astray but have the buffers of income, and power and influence. Healing them should be a relatively easy task.

When the stories of the transformations produced by today's Josephs are brought to light we will begin to seek them out as a source of healing and a balm for our most critical wounds—from blighted urban areas to the suburbs where young people drift aimlessly into destructive and self-destructive behavior.

I believe that even those who may not have the capacity to understand or truly value and appreciate the role that the Josephs can play will still be willing to support them because of the financial and material benefits that will come from the social stability they produce. And I believe that, in time, even those individuals who are attracted only by such external benefits that the Josephs can bring will come to appreciate the deeper value they have. As these individuals become engaged with the Josephs, they will gradually come to understand the healing properties that the Josephs have. Once they enter the "gravitational field" of our Josephs, I am confident they will see what I have seen.

This was my experience. I don't consider myself a great scholar and I did not begin my relationship with our Josephs as a deeply religious person. I did not seek them out as a person who was longing for something that was missing in my life. I was fairly happy. And, to be honest, I do not fully comprehend the Joseph phenomenon. To this day, I don't understand how a faith-based organization can reach into the heart of the most severely damaged individual and transform him. I may not understand it but I am impressed with the evidence, which is overwhelming.

As I said, I didn't discover the power of the Josephs through any deep religious convictions or any personal unhappiness. I was just the founder of a policy institute looking at possible remedies for the problems of poverty. Then, in 1994, the National Center for Neighborhood Enterprise began hosting a series of town meetings throughout the nation. For two years, I traveled to sites in seven regions of the country and invited grassroots leaders from a five-hundred-mile radius to tell us "What Works and Why."

Time and again, I heard the same testimony from hundreds of different grassroots leaders—from the Native American reservations of New Mexico, from black grassroots leaders of inner-city neighborhoods, from whites who lived in poverty-ridden mining towns of Virginia, and from Hispanics from our nation's barrios. What they told me was that faith works.

And more important than their words, they brought evidence of their testimony. Wherever I went, I saw people who had been damaged, whose lives had been shattered, who were made whole again. This was uncontestable, empirical evidence. I talked to people who had been in prison, who had infected their own sons with drugs, who had been prostitutes, people who all of the experts said you can't do anything with, and I saw them transformed.

I met a white man who told me that for seven years he was a police officer who was addicted to violence—violence against those he arrested and violence against his own family. But he found his way to a grassroots ministry and his life was transformed. His addiction to violence disintegrated and he has been freed now for more than seven years.

I have seen firsthand remarkable examples of the healing properties and powers of modern-day Josephs, and this book is a testimony of what I have witnessed. Today, among the most devastated economic and social conditions, the embers of spiritual renewal are still alive in the work of thousands of grassroots leaders. If these embers can be nourished by those who have wealth and influence in society, the flames of revitalization will become a brushfire that will sweep across the nation, bringing life and hope where there is now only cynicism, confusion and despair.

People may ask me what evidence I have that our Josephs can stop the moral free-fall of our nation. I cannot present credentials or degrees that attest to their expertise. But I have more simple yet powerful evidence, like that of the blind man described in the New Testament.

For years, that man had no sight and spent his days as a

beggar. But then one day he went to Jesus and he was healed. The Bible said that scribes and pharisees were skeptical and tried to discredit Jesus and intimidate the man, asking him, "Do you believe He is the Messiah?" The man replied, "Oh what a marvelous thing! That you great men of wisdom and knowledge would ask me, a poor and humble man, if He is the Messiah! All I can tell you is that . . . I was blind . . . and now I see."

Epilogue

Each year, the National Center for Neighborhood Enterprise honors seven outstanding individuals who have achieved against the odds—who have challenged and overcome obstacles that surely would have defeated individuals of lesser spirit. NCNE does this not only to reward these extraordinary people, but to showcase for America the fact that low-income people not only have solutions for their own plight but have acquired insight into the human condition and devised remedies for ills that infect our society at all levels.

At the 1996 Achievement Against the Odds awards celebrations, William Schambra—a longtime friend and supporter of NCNE and director of general programs at The Lynde and Harry Bradley Foundation—gave a remarkable and even revolutionary address to an audience that ranged from grassroots leaders to top officials of the government. In words that ring with the vulnerability and sincerity of an individual who has honestly confronted his own essential being, Schambra describes what it is that grassroots leaders, uniquely, can provide for our nation.

I believe that these words, in which William Schambra so eloquently acknowledges the unique capacities of grassroots leaders, will one day be looked upon as a founding document of a broad-based movement which will unite Americans beyond differences in race, ethnicity, education, and income in a common, powerful effort to revive and revitalize our nation.

AMERICA'S ARMY OF NEIGHBORHOOD HEALERS

Remedies in Search of Resources

by William A. Schambra

The question has been asked, "How can we make grassroots groups and the work they do more "acceptable" to mainstream America?"

Now, to me, that is a paradoxical question. I consider myself a mainstream kind of guy, and I not only find grassroots groups acceptable, I just can't get enough of the personal testimonies of their accomplishments.

If Bob Woodson tells me that community leaders such as Juan Rivera, Rita Jackson, and Carl Hardrick are speaking together—if he tells me that redirected young gang members such as Geanie and Chan and "Big Bird" from Hartford are going to speak somewhere—I'm there. As a grassroots leader from Los Angeles, Leon Watkins, always remarks when he sees me, "I keep showin' up."

What is it that draws me, a mainstream guy, back again and again to these kinds of sessions? As I reflected on this question—and I reflected on it a while and I'm still thinking about it—I recalled one of my experiences recently at a Woodson gathering that I think begins to explain it.

The last time I was at a gathering with Pastor Freddie Garcia and Juan Rivera at their substance abuse program in San Antonio, Victory Fellowship, I went up to Juan and described to him, with some puzzlement and perplexity, the deep refreshment and revitalization I always took away from sessions like that, and I told him that I sensed that it was somehow related to the struggles that I faced in my own life—struggles different from his only insofar as they occurred on the streets of more fashionable neighborhoods.

Pastor Rivera, the great minister to addicts, prisoners, and prostitutes, put his hand on my shoulder and said gently, "Hey, you're one of us."

Me? Addict? Prisoner? Prostitute? You bet. I may never have been addicted to heroin or crack, but had I not, in fact, been enslaved to the other legal, so-called acceptable chemical addictions? Had I not been hopelessly addicted at various points in my life to work, to scholarly credentials, to physical appearances, to professional success, political power, social status? I may never have been a prisoner behind physical bars, but had I not been imprisoned within my own inflated ego, my exaggerated notions of who I am, what I can do, my false presuppositions and prejudices about what others can do and who they are? I may never have prostituted my body for money, but, far worse, how many times have I prostituted my spirit, my very soul, to achieve petty recognition, to win applause from the crowd, to impress a boss, to win professional advancement? I have been an addict, a prisoner, a prostitute.

What Pastor Rivera was offering me that day was infinitely more valuable than anything I could ever offer him. He was inviting me into his family, the community of the broken, the addicted, the enslaved; the community of those who had acknowledged and repented for their sin; the community of those who had found forgiveness and redemption and have summoned into their midst the healing presence of Christ.

This invitation to join the healing community of broken and redeemed children of God, that is what I sense whenever I am around the grassroots folks that Bob Woodson brings together. That is what, every time, without fail, sends me away spiritually refreshed, renewed and healed.

Now, it might seem like Pastor Rivera's invitation would be irresistible to everybody. That mainstream America would come flocking. That is hardly the case. . . . Because the critical first step in accepting that invitation involves admitting that we are indeed broken, that something is seriously wrong, and that we are helpless and our lives are out of control. Now just think of how much of our time and energy, as individuals and as a society, is devoted to preserving the illusion that nothing's wrong, that everything is OK, that everything's under control. If only we have the right IQ, go to the right school, get the right grade—if we join the right country club, join the right company—nothing can touch us. We'll be in control and in charge of our own lives and destinies.

And when things go very wrong and we're finally confronted with irrefutable evidence of brokenness, not to worry—we can always rush over to the altar of Science. Just as we seem to believe there's no physical malady that can't be cured through medicine, so we seem to think there's no emotional or spiritual malady that can't be cured through psychology or sociology or some other social science. With the help of social therapists and professionals, we human beings can still be in control. All we need is a government willing to buy us enough therapeutic experts.

Given our huge investment in the illusion of our own omnipotence, no wonder the message of grassroots leaders isn't particularly popular. You will notice their language. They don't talk about dysfunction and pathologies and being "at-risk," all of which suggest material deficiencies that can somehow be redressed by government or science. They talk, instead, about brokenness, and sin, and redemption—all of which suggest that we're helpless on our own and that we must look beyond our mere human powers if we are to be healed.

When Pastor Freddie Garcia stands before an audience of thousands in a Houston auditorium, after a group of his former addicts have performed his play, "The Junkie," he says to them, "Listen to me, folks. The miracle that took place in our lives didn't happen because we called upon the name of Socrates, Charles Darwin, Karl Marx, or Sigmund Freud. This transformation in our lives took place when we called upon the name of our Lord and Savior, Jesus Christ." What Freddie says is true—but you can imagine what that does to those of us who have spent our lives worshipfully studying Socrates, Darwin, Marx, and Freud.

Now there is one hopeful sign that indicates that the message of grassroots leaders may be listened to more carefully and more attentively in the future. Among many Americans, there is a growing awareness that there really is something fundamentally wrong with our nation today—something that forces its way through the walls of denial, something well beyond the curative powers of government, public policy, or science. You hear more and more discussion about the moral and spiritual bankruptcy of this nation. About a national sickness of the soul. Sickness doesn't just dwell in the inner city, although it may be more visible there because folks don't have the material resources that hide the effects of disastrous spiritual diseases as rich people do.

The fact is that spiritual sickness is manifest throughout society. And many Americans sense, quite properly, that the way to fight back against all this is to begin to restore the institutions of civil society. We hear more and more about the need to revitalize the so-called mediating structures of society—the family, neighborhood, church, the voluntary associations—structures that once gave form and substance to our deepest moral and spiritual convictions. In other words, to return to the message of Pastor Rivera, Americans are coming to yearn for the kind of healing community that becomes possible through the communion of the broken and repentant children of God.

Now some Americans would like to experience that sort of community, but they don't think it's possible anymore, given the advanced deterioration of our civic institutions. They're full of despair and resignation. They look at the dry and scattered bones of our families and our neighborhoods, and they say, "Surely, no one can breathe life back into these lifeless bones." Tell that to Freddie Garcia. Tell that to Juan Rivera—Leon Watkins—Carl Hardrick. Tell that to the grassroots folks that I had the great joy and pleasure of meeting in Milwaukee—Deacon Bill Lock, Lessie Handy, Cordelia Taylor.

Every day of their lives these extraordinary and remarkable men and women take the broken bodies of addicts, prisoners, and prostitutes and breathe the life of Christ back in them. They take abandoned and boarded-up homes and build joyful temples of worship. They take rundown corner taverns and build senior citizen facilities and day-care centers. They take abandoned stores and build diners. They take cast-off factories and build incubators for new businesses.

They take the empty lots and the glass-strewn streets of the inner city and rebuild healthy, vibrant, close-knit neighborhoods. They take those dry and scattered bones and rebuild the body of Christ.

Don't tell these folks that we can't revive our civic institutions. Because they have seen and they have experienced civic and spiritual death and they have seen and experienced, and now they themselves generate, civic and spiritual resurrection. If we yearn for the restoration of communities—to heal them and transform them—nobody knows better how to restore those communities than the grassroots people. Because they've done it under the least hospitable circumstances imaginable, long after everybody else—all the agencies, all the public policy experts, all the Ph.D.s—threw up their hands and said nothing more could be done.

To put it a different way, if I'm ever in a serious accident, I don't want to be treated by a professor in medical science. Get me one of those doctors who spent a lot of time in emergency rooms. That's where grassroots have been trained—in the emergency rooms of civil society. They are civic "trauma" specialists. They get the worst cases, the so-called hopeless cases. People come to them smashed, broken, bleeding, barely breathing. . . . Grassroots leaders send them back into the world healed and transformed and now capable of transforming others.

If America is prepared to undergo serious civic healing—and I sense that it is—there is no better place for us to turn for counsel and direction than to our nation's trauma specialists. And when we come to them, now with the right frame of mind, as children of God, confessing our brokenness and seeking redemption, let us bring what gifts we have to offer in exchange for their counsel and wisdom about civic restoration.

It is my sense that all over America today citizens are beginning to hear the call to go beyond their comfortable circumstances, to put themselves and their gifts in service of inner-city healers like Juan Rivera, Carl Hardrick, and Leon Watkins.

I have spoken with businessmen and professionals who have been wonderfully successful at what they do. They make a lot of money. Suddenly, they arrive at middle age and realize that something fundamental is missing. These people come to feel that they're called to offer their wealth and social skills in the service of some higher purpose. Yet they know that getting involved with big top-down private charities will not suffice, because those kinds of organizations don't fight poverty any more effectively than they create wealth. So they're searching for something else.

I have spoken with young people who tell me they want to devote themselves to a cause, to an undertaking that will give their lives a real sense of meaning and purpose. Yes, there are such young people today even in these jaded and cynical times! All the great secular ideologies, which in previous decades might have spoken to that youthful yearning, have dried up and collapsed. They proved to be gods that failed. These young people are still searching for something else.

And I have spoken with quietly faithful Christians who, at some point or another in their lives, find themselves living the experience of Jacob. Like Jacob, they found themselves alone in their tent one night, in the dark night of the soul, wrestling with their angel. For some, it was an addiction or alcohol dependency. For others, it was the tragic death of a loved one, or losing a job, or a divorce. With the grace of God, they came away from those struggles, blessed, like Jacob. But, like Jacob who was smitten on the thigh, they will forever walk with a limp. No longer are they into appearances, or into facades of perfection, or in denial. They are searching for something else. They are searching for a community of people who, like them, have reached an awareness of a new meaning in life, though they now walk with a limp.

Let all of those searchers after servanthood now bring their wealth, their professional skills, their dedication, their energy, their humble and open hearts, and offer them as gifts to our faithful grassroots leaders as we seek their assistance and counsel in the restoration of our nation through a healing community.

If we are to rebuild our nation's civic institutions, then, in every city and community throughout this nation, our faith-based grassroots leaders must be invited to sit down with those who have heeded the call to servanthood and, with the help of a group such as the National Center for Neighborhood Enterprise, must join together to work out the terms of a mutually beneficial and fulfilling relationship.

Grassroots leaders have been able to accomplish so much in their neighborhoods with virtually nothing by way of assistance and support from the larger society. Just imagine what might be possible if we were able to afford this new alliance—an alliance between resources in search of service and servants in search of resources!

And note that all of this can happen beginning now, beginning today. None of this depends on passing laws, or winning elections, or raising or lowering taxes, or persuading some stubborn government bureaucrat to cooperate. This is civil society, using its own spiritual and moral resources to heal itself. All that is required is for us, one by one, to start heeding God's call to his children to confess their brokenness and come together in community.

If we form this communion, not only will our low-income communities revive, and not only will our civic institutions rise from the ashes, but more and more so-called mainstream Americans will experience the same healing and transformation that I have always found in joyful gatherings such as this one today.

Indeed, I am still drawing sustenance, and insight, and healing, from the moment that Pastor Juan Rivera put his hand on my shoulder and said simply, "Hey, you're one of us."

William Schambra, a longtime friend of NCNE, is Director of General Programs for the Lynde and Harry Bradley Foundation in Milwaukee. He has served as senior adviser and chief speech writer for Attorney General Edwin Meese III, Director of the Office of the White House Office of Personnel Management, Constance Horner, and Secretary of Health and Human Services Louis Sullivan. He has also served as Director of Social Policy Programs for the American Enterprise Institute (AEI) and co-director of AEI's "A Decade of Study of the Constitution" and has written extensively on the Constitution, community revitalization, and civil society.

Notes

CHAPTER 1: DREAMS AND OMENS OF IMPENDING DOOM

1. Avis Thomas-Lester, "A Generation Lost: Violence Haunts D.C. Woman Whose Children Were Slain, One by One," *Washington Post,* June 30, 1996.
2. John Sibley Butler and Charles C. Moskos, *All That We Can Be: Black Leadership and Racial Integration the Army Way* (New York: Basic Books, 1996).
3. USA Today/CNN/Gallup Poll of 1,001 adults conducted May 9–12, 1996.
4. Thomas M. Burton, "How a Yogurt Company Developed a New Cancer Drug," *Wall Street Journal,* July 17, 1996.
5. Genesis 37–41.

CHAPTER 2: CONSPIRACY IN THE PHARAOH'S COURT

1. William J. Raspberry, "Civil Rights Gains Bypassing Poorest Negroes," *Washington Post,* October 31, 1965.
2. Michael G. Franc, "What Americans Think About Education," *Issues 94,* Heritage Foundation, Washington, D.C., 1994.
3. Joseph G. Conti and Brad Stetson, *A New Black Vanguard,* (Westport, CT: Praeger Publishers, 1993).

4. Gerald F. Seib and Joe Davidson, "Shades of Gray," *Wall Street Journal,* September 29, 1994.

5. E. L. Thornbrough, ed., *Booker T. Washington* (Englewood Cliffs, N.J.: Prentice Hall, 1969), p. 57.

6. William Raspberry, "When Push Comes to Shove," *Washington Post,* August 29, 1990, p. A25.

7. Linda Chavez, "Minorities Can't Measure Up?" *USA Today,* February 15, 1995.

8. Morton Kondracke, "Precarious Course for Affirmative Action," *Washington Post.*

9. Mary Jordan, "Chavis Used NAACP Money to Settle a Legal Dispute, *Washington Post,* July 29, 1994.

10. "NAACP Audit Finds Lavish Spending," *Washington Times,* July 14, 1995, p. 8.

11. Clint Bolick and Mark Liedl, "Fulfilling America's Promise," *Heritage Backgrounder* no. 773 (June 1990), Heritage Foundation, Washington, D.C.

12. *Up from Dependency,* a report of the U.S. Domestic Policy Council, Low-Income Opportunity Working Group, under the auspices of the Inter-agency Low-Income Opportunity Advisory Board, 1986, Figure 5, p. 15.

13. Ibid., pp. 12–14.

14. John McKnight, *The Careless Society* (New York: Basic Books, 1995), pp. 108–109.

15. Stuart Butler and Anna Kondratas, *Out of the Poverty Trap* (New York: Free Press, 1987), pp. 11–12.

16. Michael K. Brown and Stephen P. Erie, "Blacks and the Legacy of the Great Society: The Economic and Political Impact of Federal Social Policy," *Public Policy,* vol. 12 (Summer 1981), quoted in Charles Murray, *Losing Ground* (New York: Basic Books, 1984), p. 87.

17. Robert B. Hill, "The Black Family: Building on Strengths," in *On the Road to Economic Freedom: An Agenda for Black Progress,* ed. Robert L. Woodson, Sr. (Washington, D.C.: Regnery Gateway, 1987), p. 89.

18. Niara Sudarkasa, "An Exposition of the Value Premises Underlying Black Family Studies," *Journal of the National Medical Association,* vol. 67, no. 3 (August 16, 1972): 237.

19. Robert B. Hill, *Informal Adoption among Black Families* (Washington, D.C.: National Urban League, 1977).

20. Evaxx, Inc., "A Study of Black Americans' Attitudes Toward Self-Help," unpublished report prepared for the American Enterprise Institute, August 1981.

21. Toni Locy, "Federal Court Seizes Control of D.C. Child Welfare System, *Washington Post,* May 23, 1995, p. A1.

22. Connie Field and Marilyn Mulford, Clarity Educational Productions, Inc., "Freedom on My Mind," produced for PBS, *The American Experience,* aired January 15, 1996.

23. August Meier and Elliott Rudwick, *From Plantation to Ghetto* (New York: Hill and Wang, 1966), pp. 138–139.

24. Scott Ellsworth, *Death in a Promised Land* (Baton Rouge: Louisiana State University Press, 1982, 1992).

25. Philip Murphy, "Black Flight: Years of Liberal Government Drive Away D.C.'s Middle Class," *Policy Review,* no. 72 (April 1, 1995), Heritage Foundation, Washington, D.C., p. 28.

26. Colbert I. King, "While the Mayor Smiles," *Washington Post,* July 8, 1995, p. 28.

27. Hamil Harris, "At D.C. Morgue, Foulness and Filth," *Washington Post,* May 25, 1996, p. 1.

28. Amy Goldstein, "Mental Health Provider in State of Chaos," *Washington Post,* May 28, 1996, p. 1.

29. HUD Office of the Inspector General, "Multi-Region Audit of the Comprehensive Improvement Assistance Program," Audit Report #90-TS-101-0009, April 6, 1990.

30. HUD Office of Public and Indian Housing, "New Jersey Strike Force Report."

31. HUD Office of Public and Indian Housing, "Troubled PHA Profile Screens," September 30, 1990.

32. HUD, "Multi-Region Audit," p. 6.

33. HUD, "Troubled PHA Profile Screens."

CHAPTER 3: A HISTORY SUPPRESSED BY THE PHARAOH'S ADVISERS

1. Loren Schweninger, *Black Property Owners in the South: 1790–1915* (Champaign: University of Illinois Press, 1990).
2. Walter Williams, "When There Is a Will to Overcome," *Washington Times*, August 16, 1995, Syndicated by Creators, Inc., Los Angeles.
3. Robert Higgs, *Competition and Coercion* (Cambridge, England: Cambridge University Press, 1977), p. 134.
4. James M. McPherson, *The Abolitionist Legacy* (Chichester, N.J.: Princeton University Press, 1975), p. 222.
5. Ibid.
6. Elizabeth Wright, "Keeping the Spotlight on Failure," *Issues & Views*, vol. 9, no. 1 (Winter 1993), pp. 3–4.
7. John Sibley Butler, *Entrepreneurship and Self-Help Among Black Americans: A Reconsideration of Race and Economics* (Albany: State University of New York Press, 1991), p. 147.
8. John Sibley Butler, Preface to the Alliance of Historical Black Colleges and Universities Schools of Business Case Series (unpublished).
9. Louis R. Harlan, *Booker T. Washington: The Wizard of Tuskegee* (New York: Oxford University Press, 1972).
10. S. B. Fuller, President, Fuller Products Company, to the National Association of Manufacturers, December 6, 1963.
11. Cynthia Tucker, "Free to Think What You Will," *Atlanta Constitution*, July 31, 1994, p. R5.

CHAPTER 4: MODERN-DAY JOSEPHS

1. Freddie and Ninfa Garcia, *Outcry in the Barrio*, Freddie Garcia Ministries, San Antonio, Tex., 1988.

CHAPTER 5: JOSEPH AND PHARAOH

1. Richard L. Barclay, "The Poor, I Hire Them," *Wall Street Journal*, May 24, 1995, p A14.
2. John McKnight, *The Careless Society, Community and Its Counterfeits* (New York: Basic Books, 1995). pp. 6–7.

P55 - Block Values